Energy Law in Georgia

Energy Law in Georgia

Second Edition

Irakli Samkharadze
Irakli Pkhakadze
Zurab Gomiashvili

This book was originally published as a monograph in the International Encyclopaedia of Laws/Energy Law.

Founding Editor: Roger Blanpain
General Editor: Frank Hendrickx
Volume Editors: Kurt Deketelaere & Bram Delvaux

Wolters Kluwer

Published by:
Kluwer Law International B.V.
PO Box 316
2400 AH Alphen aan den Rijn
The Netherlands
E-mail: lrs-sales@wolterskluwer.com
Website: www.wolterskluwer.com/en/solutions/kluwerlawinternational

Sold and distributed by:
Wolters Kluwer Legal & Regulatory U.S.
920 Links Avenue
Landisville, PA 17538
United States of America
E-mail: customer.service@wolterskluwer.com

ISBN 978-94-035-3497-8

e-Book: ISBN 978-94-035-3507-4
web-PDF: ISBN 978-94-035-3517-3

The Author

Dr Irakli Samkharadze (born on 31 January 1989), an Associate Professor in International Law, the Head of European Integration Research Centre at Georgian National University, Postdoctoral Researcher at the Free University of Berlin, has earned his PhD in Law from the Faculty of Law of Tbilisi State University, Georgia. Within his doctoral research, he has worked as an International Scholar at KU Leuven's Institute for Environmental and Energy Law (Belgium) as well as DAAD Research Fellow at the Energy Law Institute of Friedrich-Schiller University of Jena (Germany). He holds an LLM in International and European Public Law from Erasmus University Rotterdam, The Netherlands and an MA in Constitutional Law from Tbilisi State University. He has proven experience in cross-border project management, advisory, and consultancy services commissioned by the European Union (EU), Energy Community (EnC), United Nations Development Programme, development banks and other donors. In his current position within the German energy consulting company – OMNIA, he supports partners in designing, implementing, and navigating the legislative and regulatory landscape for sustainable, competitive, transparent, and efficient energy markets. He teaches Energy Law, EU Law and Theory of Law courses at Ivane Javakhishvili Tbilisi State University and Ilia State University, Georgia. Irakli is a recipient of a number of academic scholarships, and, among other things, he frequently speaks at international conferences and contributes to conventional and online publications. He is connected and deeply embedded in the international community of energy law and climate change.

The Author

Co-Authors

Mr Irakli Pkhakadze (born on 7 July 1997) is a law graduate, holding a degree with Honours from Ilia State University, Georgia. He has studied at the University of Groningen, The Netherlands, on LLB in International and European Union Law, within the European Union's Erasmus + exchange programme. Mr Irakli is currently pursuing his studies at The University of Oslo, LLM in Information and Communication Technology Law, Norway, and EULISP IT/IP Law at the University of Hannover, Germany.

He has decent professional experience working in law firms (incl. Associate Lawyer at LLC Solutions 2.0) as a practising paralegal, assistant, and lawyer. Throughout his studies, he has been actively participating in a number of international projects, conferences, and moot courts. As the future leader, in January 2020, he paid a visit to the governmental and legislative bodies of Japan with the official invitation of the Ministry of Foreign Affairs of Japan. Along with a number of certifications, Irakli is a holder of various academic scholarships.

Mr Zurab Gomiashvili (born on 21 December 1994) is a law graduate from Ilia State University, Georgia. Zurab has pursued his LLM studies in Environmental Law at Stockholm University, Sweden. Zurab has participated in several academic conferences held by national and/or international legal entities and attended moot courts in Civil and International Humanitarian Law. He started his professional career as a corporate lawyer, and since then, he has worked as a legal assistant in the fields of administrative law, constitutional law, European law and public international law.

Co-Authors

Table of Contents

Table of Contents

Table of Contents

List of Abbreviations

AA	EU-Georgia Association Agreement
BUR	Biennial Update Report
CCC	Climate Change Council
CP	Contracting Party
DCFTA	Agreement on Deep and Comprehensive Free Trade Area
DSO	Distribution System Operator
EaP	Eastern Partnership Initiative
EC	European Commission
EGD	European Green Deal
EIA	Environmental Impact Assessment
EIEC	Environmental Information and Education Centre
EnC	Energy Community
EnCT	Treaty Establishing the Energy Community
ENP	European Neighbourhood Policy
EPG	Energo-Pro Georgia
EU	European Union
F-gas	Fluorinated Greenhouse Gas
GAA	Georgian American Alloys
GeoStat	National Statistics Office of Georgia
GHG	Greenhouse Gas
GNERC	Georgian National Energy and Water Supply Regulatory Commission
GoG	Government of Georgia
GOGC	Georgian Oil and Gas Corporation
INDC	Intended Nationally Determined Contribution
KP	Kyoto Protocol
LEPL	Legal Entity of Public Law
MoEPA	Ministry of Environmental Protection and Agriculture of Georgia
MoESD	Ministry of Economy and Sustainable Development of Georgia
MP	Montreal Protocol

List of Abbreviations

MW	Mega Watt
NECP	National Energy and Climate Plan
NEEAP	National Energy Efficiency Action Plan
NOC	National Oil Company
ODS	Ozone Depleting Substances
OU	Ownership Unbundling
PA	Paris Agreement
RES	Renewable Energy Sources
SAOG	The State Agency for Oil and Gas
SEA	Strategic Environmental Assessment
SOCAR	State Oil Company of Azerbaijan Republic
TPA	Third-Party Access
TSO	Transmission System Operator
UN	United Nations
UNFCCC	United Nations Framework Convention on Climate Change
WREP	Western Route Export Pipeline

Preface

Albeit the last couple of years have seen a growing interest in energy law scholarship in Georgia, it is still considered a new area of law emerging at an accelerated pace and receiving more attention in academic literature. Georgia's energy law evolution is guided by a variety of developments, one of which is the EU's strong impact on transformation of the country's energy sector. Rethinking its energy policy, Georgia has endeavoured to modernize its obsolete energy regulatory framework under the footprint of the EU standards and strengthen its energy relations with the EU and other key stakeholders in the region. The 2017 Membership to the EnC is a topical example of adding another thick layer to the process of Europeanization of Georgia's energy law and policy, when the application of the EU's energy *acquis* transcends national borders and is transposed onto the Georgian energy regulatory regimes.

Against this backdrop, the present monograph – an overview of the legal and regulatory framework of energy sector – traces the development of Georgia's energy law and engages in describing the core pillars of Georgian national energy law and policy. In doing so, first and foremost, the monograph provides a general introduction to the topic by describing the country's key energy legislation and their historical development, providing an overview of the basics of energy sector, the role of governmental institutions, and the sources of energy law in the country's legal system. On top of that, the monograph scrutinizes the regulatory systems of electricity, gas, petrol and engages deeply in exploiting greener energy standards in the country, such as laws on energy efficiency and renewable energy. The last two parts of this contribution are dedicated to exploring the interplay between energy law and environmental law as well as climate change, as fast-emerging sub-disciplines of energy law. Along with existing national legislation, the monograph largely covers international legislation and treaties along with EU energy and climate *acquis* gradually becoming an integral part of Georgian domestic legislation.

Dr Irakli Samkharadze
Berlin, Germany
29 June 2023

Acknowledgements

The author expresses his deepest gratitude to the Volume Editors Professor Dr Kurt Deketelaere and Dr Bram Delvaux for their kind invitation and the most inspiring lectures and talks in Leuven, Belgium prior to the commencement of the work on this monograph.

Acknowledgements

Disclaimer

This outline of energy law in Georgia and the views expressed herein are the personal opinions of the author & co-authors and can in no way be taken to reflect the position of the International Encyclopaedia of Laws.

Disclaimer

General Introduction

Chapter 1. Introduction

§1. Geography and Population

1. Georgia (Georgian 'Sakartvelo') is a country in the South Caucasus region located at the crossroads of Western Asia and Eastern Europe. Situated strategically, to the west, Georgia is surrounded by the Black Sea, to the north by Russia, to the south by Turkey and Armenia, and to the southeast by Azerbaijan. Georgia has a total area of 69,700 km^2, and its approximate population is about 3.718 million inhabitants.

2. Georgia includes three ethnic enclaves: Abkhazia, in the northwest (principal city Sokhumi); Ajaria, in the southwest (principal city Batumi); and South Ossetia, in the north (principal city Tskhinvali). Tbilisi is the capital and the biggest city of Georgia followed by Kutaisi and Batumi, as the second and the third largest cities by their territory and population. 'Georgia' is the name of the state of Georgia, while Georgian is the official language of Georgia, and, in the Autonomous Republic of Abkhazia, also Abkhazian. The official language as well as the state flag, the coat of arms, and the anthem of Georgia are established and protected by the organic law of Georgia.[1]

3. Georgia's main natural resources include water and forests. The total annual runoff of rivers in West Georgia exceeds three times that of rivers in East Georgia. About eight-hundred and fifty small lakes and over forty reservoirs with irrigation and hydro energy function are registered on the territory of the country. Georgia is rich in underground waters, and there are mineral and thermal waters. Forests occupy about 40% of the territory of Georgia with a total wood resource of 443 million m^3. Over eight hundred species of plants are registered in forests, among which, in particular, in reserves of West Georgia are several relic and endemic species. Additionally, the country has coal deposits, petroleum and a variety of other resources ranging from peat to marble.[2]

1. Article 2(4), No. 786 Constitution of Georgia, 24 Aug. 1995.
2. Third National Communication of Georgia to the UN Framework Convention on Climate Change (UNFCCC).

§2. LEGAL AND POLITICAL STRUCTURE

4. According to the Georgian Constitution, Georgia is a democratic republic and people are the source of State authority.[3] The most recent revision of the Constitution relates to the 2017–2018 Constitutional Reform marking the transition from a presidential to a parliamentary system, re-establishment of classic constitutional institutions and amendment of the whole body of the Constitution aiming at modifying the concept of regulating human rights and freedoms.[4] Georgia currently is a unitary parliamentary republic, with the Government elected through a representative democracy. The legislation of Georgia complies with the universally recognized principles and norms of international law. An international treaty of Georgia takes precedence over domestic normative acts unless it comes into conflict with the Constitution or the Constitutional Agreement of Georgia.[5]

5. In the aftermath of disintegration of the Soviet Union, Georgia restored political independence, charted a course towards European integration and started conducting reforms in all spheres of cooperation between the European Union (EU) and Georgia. To date, the country participates in the European Neighborhood Policy (ENP) and in a specific eastern dimension of ENP – the Eastern Partnership Initiative (EaP), both political formats for expanding Europeanization. The conclusion of the EU-Georgia Association Agreement (AA) in 2014 alluded to the process of Europeanization in a much more cautious tone requiring a higher degree of approximation (i.e., convergence of laws and policy goals) along with political association, including in the field of energy law.[6] The constituent part of the AA is an 'Agreement on Deep and Comprehensive Free Trade Area' (DCFTA), which opens up the way for goods and services produced in Georgia to the EU internal market and increases the investment attractiveness.

6. Georgian law, descended from the principles of Romano-Germanic law, is generally divided into public *(jus publicum)* and private *(jus privatum)* laws. Public law mainly comprises constitutional, administrative and criminal laws as well as customs, taxation and procedure legislation. Traditionally, civil and corporate law disciplines fell under the scope of private law. Although such a division still retains its practical importance for the classification of legal acts and the identification of the course of justice, the Georgian legal system witnesses the rise of more specialized subjects that lie in between public and private law boundaries, namely energy law, climate law, media law, labour law and health law.

7. The structure of judicial power in Georgia is articulated by the Constitution of Georgia and the respective primary and secondary laws thereof. Private law disputes are adjudicated under civil proceedings on an adversarial basis, while public

3. Article 3(2), No. 786 Constitution of Georgia, 24 Aug. 1995.
4. *See* I. Samkharadze, *Text of the Constitution of Georgia* (International Encyclopedia of Laws: Constitutional Law, Wolters Kluwer, Kluwer Law International, Suppl. 154), 2020.
5. Article 4(5), No. 934 Law of Georgia on International Treaties of Georgia, 16 Oct. 1997.
6. *See* I. Samkharadze,. *Europeanization of Energy Law and Policy Beyond the Member States: The Case of Georgia*, 130 Elsevier Energy Pol'y J. 1–6 (2019).

law cases are disputed under administrative proceedings. The constitutional supervision is carried out by the Constitutional Court of Georgia protecting the constitutional rights of individuals and settling disputes between public institutions. Georgian case law reveals no real traces of referring to the Association Agreement and the judgment of the European Court of Justice. At the time of writing, one of the rarest references to the AA was made in 2015, when the Constitutional Court of Georgia based its reasoning on Articles 228 and 229 of the AA.[7]

§3. Social and Economic Characteristics

8. Georgia aspires to develop a competitive private sector and, therefore, ensures Government's minimal entrepreneurial involvement in it. Undoubtedly, highly competitive, liberalized, modern, stable and secure energy infrastructure is strongly intertwined with the idea of socio-economic development, though the country's major energy resources are largely unexploited. Subscribing to the universal European values, gradual economic integration with the EU has become the centrepiece of Georgia's socio-economic development. To date, Georgia's economic policy is defined by three main principles.

9. The first principle implies ensuring fast and efficient economic growth driven by the development of real (production) sector of the economy, which will resolve economic problems that exist in the country, create jobs and reduce poverty.[8]

10. The second principle relies on the implementation of economic policies that facilitate inclusive economic growth – it envisages universal involvement of the population in the economic development process (including diaspora, migrants, ethnic minorities and other groups), prosperity for each member of society through economic growth, their social equality and improvement of the living standards of the population.[9]

11. The third main principle of an economic policy is based on rational use of natural resources, ensuring environmental safety and sustainability and avoiding natural disasters during the process of economic development.[10]

12. By integrating the aims and purposes identified in the Socio-Economic Policy, dependence on the energy market for import should be purposefully reduced, and the improvement of the investment environment will be directly proportional to the growing development of the energy market. In addition to this, it is crucial to highlight how significant public-private partnership schemes in the energy sector are, in terms of investment, an impetus for the energy environment and stability.

---

7. S. Blockmans et al., *Integrity and Judicial Reform on Trial*, in *The Struggle for Good Governance in Eastern Europe* 122 (M. Emerson, D. Cenusa, T. Kovziridze & V. Movchan (eds), Centre for European Policy Studies 2018).
8. Social-economic Development Strategy of Georgia 'GEORGIA 2020', 3.
9. *Ibid.*
10. *Ibid.*

§4. Energy Sector

13. The energy sector in Georgia is of the highest economic, social and geopolitical importance. Adding to its major hydroelectric capacity, in recent years, there have been large investments in oil and gas pipeline connections with Azerbaijan, transiting onto Turkey and across the Black Sea. These have also assured Georgia's higher degree of energy independence from Russia resulting in the emergence of the country as a regional transit hub.[11] An inefficient and corrupt energy system was substantially reformed and restructured starting in 2004, and the country moved from a state of frequent blackouts to a condition where it attracts sizeable foreign direct investment and exports electricity to all its neighbours.[12]

14. The first few years of the formation of an independent, market-based economic system in the early 1990s were particularly difficult for Georgia due to civil unrest, armed conflicts in Abkhazia and South Ossetia, energy and transport blockades, extremely high crime rates, severed economic ties, the loss of old traditional markets and suppliers, and high rates of workforce migration. It has led to unprecedented economic stagnation, hyperinflation and a huge increase in unemployment.

15. This has naturally affected Georgia's energy sector. It was not long ago when Georgia was facing a catastrophic energy crisis, such as a severe energy deficit, outdated energy infrastructures, massive natural gas shortages and electricity blackouts. Such events contributed to the total collapse of the Georgian energy legal system. Therefore, the modernization of an obsolete national energy legislative infrastructure requires a so-called paradigm shift in legal thinking and a consistent course of reform in the energy sector.

16. This course of reform is now largely driven by the partnership between the EU and the Government of Georgia (GoG) and impacts the harmonization of Georgia's energy regulatory framework under the footprint of EU legislation.[13] Transposing EU energy legislation onto Georgia's domestic legal system is the 'remedy' for Georgia to systemize its ill-regulated energy sector. This transposition, however, on the other hand, presents considerable challenges to the country and uncovers substantial legal gaps.

17. This process is smoothened with the country's integration into the European energy institutions and forums. In 2009, Georgia joined the Energy Security Multilateral Platform of the Eastern Partnership. Since 2010, Georgia has been a member of the International Renewable Energy Agency. In 2015, Georgia chaired the European Energy Charter, while in 2017, the country acceded to the Energy Community (EnC) Treaty.

---

11. M. Emerson & T. Kovziridze (eds), *Deepening EU-Georgian Relations What Why and How?* 138 (Centre for European Policy Studies 2d ed. 2018).
12. *Ibid.*
13. *See*, I. Samkharadze, *The Impact of EU Energy Law External Action on Georgian Legislation*, 1 Tbilisi State U. L. Rev. (2018).

§5. Legal Approximation

18. As early as 1997, the Parliament of Georgia adopted the No. 828 resolution on Harmonization of Georgian Legislation with the EU Law.[14] This has marked the early days of Georgia's endeavour to harmonize its domestic legislation in accordance with the EU norms and standards. Since then, many developments have taken place up until the signature of the AA. Within the framework of the Association Agreement, Georgia has amended quite a substantial number of legislative acts and/or adopted new legal acts. In particular, within the period of three years (2014–2017), nine new laws have been adopted, up to seventy laws have been amended and up to twenty-four by-laws have also been issued.

19. Legal harmonization amounts to the assimilation of legal standards and norms through the massive diffusion and transposition of foreign norms. It is aimed at the coexistence of different legal systems and the creation of an organically uniform legal system within the country. Harmonization of specific laws (as opposed to harmonization of whole legal systems) may necessitate the deployment of as little as a single transplant between different legal systems. To this end, Georgia's energy legislation harmonization must be seen as the adaptation of domestic energy law norms to the EU standards. This is carried out by legislative activities aimed at reducing the legal regulatory variance between the municipal law of Georgia and the EU energy law.

20. Legal approximation to the European standards set out in the EU regulations cannot be the subject of identical transportation, but provisions should be harmonized and adapted to the national circumstances. Transposition of a specific provision is a separate legislative activity and should not be identified as a mere translation of an EU-adopted norm. This applies to the EU energy and climate *acquis*, which must also be exported creatively to enhance their productivity and general capacity within the national legal system. Starting from the Constitution of Georgia followed by the 'Law of Georgia on Normative Acts' and 'Law of Georgia on International Treaties' the solid legal basis is created for effective harmonization of Georgian laws in several fields of action, including energy and climate change.

---

14. No. 828 The Resolution of the Parliament of Georgia 'On Harmonization of Georgian Legislation with the EU Law', 2 Sep. 1997.

Chapter 2. Basic Terms and Principles of Energy Law

§1. Historical Development

21. Georgia's energy law is in the process of constant reform and transition. Under such circumstances, there is an overlap with the legislation developed before and after the reforms. During the past decades, Georgia's energy sector has seen a major transformation. For more than twenty years, the sector was governed by the overarching 1997 Law of Georgia on Electricity and Natural Gas,[15] while the domestic energy regulatory framework included the secondary normative acts and other legislation adopted by the GoG and Georgian National Energy and Water Supply Regulatory Commission (GNERC).

22. On 20 December 2019, Georgia adopted a new framework law in energy 'Law of Georgian on Energy and Water supply' (hereinafter 'the law' or 'framework energy law'), which is to be considered a key milestone in reforming energy sector mandated by Third Energy Package (2009).[16] Georgia is not yet obliged to fully endorse the EU's so-called Winter Package influenced by the landmark United Nations Framework Convention on Climate Change (UNFCCC) of the Paris Agreement (PA). However, it should also be noted that the shift from the Third to Clean Energy (for all Europeans) Package to some degree becomes mandatory followed by the latest development at the EnC level. In November 2021, five key legislative acts were adopted by the EnC Ministerial Council with binding applicability to Georgia.[17] According to the latest 20th Ministerial Council meeting taking place on 15 December 2022, new *acquis* has also been added to the body of the energy community laws including ambitious 2030 targets for greenhouse gas emissions reduction, energy efficiency and renewable energy as well as incorporating the system for monitoring, reporting and verification (MRV).[18]

23. The framework energy law substitutes the existing market framework and creates the space, which accommodates the EU's key energy law principles and establishes the legal grounds for long-term energy strategy and planning. Thus, the legal act encapsulates the provisions of the EU energy law on unbundling Third-Party Access (TPA), regulatory authorities, consumer protection, and public service obligations to be explained in detail in the forthcoming chapters of this monograph.

24. Along with the framework energy law, Georgia has adopted sector-specific 'Law of Georgia on Encouraging the Production and Use of Energy from Renewable Sources'. The legal act sets a renewable energy target, as the renewable energy law, among other things, introduces the increase in the share of renewable energy

15. Repealed by No. 5646 Law of Georgia on Energy and Water Supply, 20 Dec. 2019.
16. For more information, *see*: https://ec.europa.eu/energy/en/topics/markets-and-consumers/market-legislation/third-energy-package, accessed on 14 Jan. 2020.
17. Energy Community Adopts Clean Energy Package, *see*: https://www.energy-community.org/news/Energy-Community-News/2021/11/30.html, accessed on 5 Jan. 2022.
18. For more detailed overview, *see*: https://www.energy-community.org/events/2022/12/MC.html, accessed on 24 Jun. 2023.

up to 35% in the gross final energy consumption for 2030. The country has a significant potential for the development of renewable energy, which remains largely untapped. According to the Aggregated Energy Balance of Georgia for 2018, renewable energy accounted for around 24% of the total primary energy supply, where hydro accounted – 17.7%, biofuels (mainly wood) and waste – 5.6% and others – 0.6%. Further utilization of Renewable Energy Sources (RES) could significantly contribute to climate change mitigation, while diversification towards other renewable generation sources besides hydro (wind, solar, geothermal, etc.) could contribute to affordability, reliability and sustainability of renewable energy supply. In that sense, the necessary legislative and policy framework (focusing on power system flexibility) of diversification in Georgia should be explored.

25. One of the latest chapters on Georgia's energy law reform includes the adoption of the package of energy efficiency laws in compactivity with the EU's energy efficiency *acquis*.[19] In December 2019, Georgia passed the Law of Georgia on Energy Labelling on the indication by labelling and providing standard product information regarding the consumption of energy and other resources by energy-related products.[20] On 21 May 2020, the Parliament of Georgia adopted two new legal acts – the Law on Energy Efficiency and the Law on Energy Performance of Buildings. These new laws constitute part of the reform of the energy sector, and it is a crucial achievement for Georgia as until 2020, it had basically no energy efficiency regulations in place and very limited investment in energy performance.

§2. The Role of the Government Institutions in Shaping Energy Law and Policy

26. Clearly, the implementation of energy policy goals at the functional level depends on government institutions developing and implementing specific action plans and actions. In this regard, there are three main government institutions in Georgia that are shaping energy law and policy, namely: Ministry of Economy and Sustainable Development of Georgia (MoESD), Ministry of Environmental Protection and Agriculture of Georgia (MoEPA), Climate Change Council (CCC) established on 23 January 2020 by No. 54 Decree of the GoG.[21]

27. Generally speaking, the main role attributed to the MoESD is to define the development, implementation and coordination of measures necessary for the sustainable development of the country; encourage forms of resource-saving production; encourage and coordinate energy efficiency measures in the fields of manufacturing, construction, transport and services; taking the necessary measures to encourage the green economy.

19. Energy Efficiency https://ec.europa.eu/energy/topics/energy-efficiency_en, accessed on 12 Sep. 2020.
20. No. 5688 Law of Georgia on Energy Labeling, 20 Dec. 2019.
21. No. 54 Decree of the Government of Georgia, 23 Dec. 2020.

28. MoESD is the core operating institution that develops and defines the country's energy priorities and strategic orientation. The Ministry develops a regulatory legal framework and defines the following as the main directions of Georgia's energy policy: (a) diversification of energy supply sources, optimal utilization of Georgia's energy resources and creation of reserves; (b) utilization of Georgia's renewable energy resources; (c) gradual approximation of Georgian legislation with EU legislation; (d) development of the Georgian energy market and improvement of the energy trade mechanism; (e) Georgia – Regional Center for Clean Energy Production and Trade in this energy; (f) development and implementation of a unified approach to energy efficiency; (g) consideration of environmental components in the implementation of energy projects; (h) improvement in the quality of services and protecting the interests of customers.[22]

29. MoESD additionally puts an Energy Efficiency Action Plan for the National Renewable Energy Action Plan. It should be noted that by the Decree of the GoG No. 186 of 7 February 2014, the MoESD has been tasked with overall coordination and monitoring of the implementation of the Association Agreement, Part of the DCFTA.

30. MoEPA is another governmental institution, which has a direct applicability to energy topics. The relevant areas of expertise include protecting the environment and managing and promoting agricultural and rural development. In particular, the following tasks of the MoEPA become crucial in achieving a comprehensive energy policy, especially in realization of green energy endeavours: (1) managing and controlling the field of use of natural resources (except minerals, oil and gas) by the state;[23] (2) promoting the principles of sustainable development and green economy in the country;[24] (3) organizing and monitoring environmental pollution;[25] (4) preparing and implementing strategic documents in the field of environmental protection and agriculture;[26] (5) developing and implementing state policy in the field of protection of atmospheric air, management and protection of water and land resources and climate change.[27]

31. In January 2020, an inter-agency coordination unit named CCC was set up under the recently passed Decree No. 54 by the GoG. The council has a mandate of establishing thematic working groups related to the climate change policy implementation area. The CCC was established in Georgia under the UNFCCC (which

---

22. Resolution of the Parliament of Georgia on the main directions of the state policy in the field of energy of Georgia.
23. Article 2(2)(b), No. 12112 Resolution of the Government of Georgia 'On the Approval of the Statute of the Ministry of Environment Protection and Agriculture of Georgia'.
24. Article 2(2)(c), *ibid.*
25. Article 2(2)(d), *ibid.*
26. Article 2(2)(m), *ibid.*
27. Article 2(2)(f), *ibid.*

aims to stabilize the concentration of Greenhouse Gases (GHGs) in the atmosphere), the Kyoto Protocol (KP – which aims to quantify GHG emissions and promote sustainable development) and the PA (which aims to strengthen the global response to climate change threats) to ensure the effective implementation of the requirements.[28]

32. According to Article 1 of the Governance Charter of the CCC, it is established to ensure the efficient implementation of the UNFCCC (the purpose of the Convention is the stabilization of GHG concentrations in the atmosphere causing climate change), also the KP to the Convention (the purpose of the KP is to limit the amount of GHG emissions and to promote the sustainable development) and the PA (the purpose of the PA is to strengthen the global response to the threats caused by climate change).

33. CCC, *inter alia,* addresses the request of establishing a relevant task force for the purpose of implementing the Sustainable Energy and Climate Change Action Plan and instructs the coordination team members to submit information biannually in accordance with the rules and procedures for the sustainable energy and climate change projects.[29]

§3. Sources of Energy Law in Georgia

34. Energy Law in Georgia is regulated by a series of laws characterized by different degrees of legal nature. The system is headed by the recently adopted primary law of Georgia on Energy and Water Supply.[30] The law establishes a general legal framework for the generation, transmission, distribution, supply of and trade in electricity, and for the transmission, distribution, supply, storage of and trade in natural gas with a view to the facilitated emergence, opening, development and integration of well-functioning, transparent and competitive electricity and natural gas markets in Georgia.[31] It also lays down the rules relating to the governing, organizing, regulating, monitoring and supervising electricity and natural gas sectors, open access to electricity and natural gas markets, cross-border exchanges in electricity and natural gas, the criteria and procedures applicable to calls for tenders and the granting of authorizations for energy activities, operation of and access to electricity and natural gas systems, public service obligations in electricity and natural gas sectors, and the rights of customers and their protection.[32]

35. Georgia's energy legal system includes other primary laws that need to be highlighted in this context. The 2019 'Law of Georgia on Encouraging the Production and Use of Energy from Renewable Sources' establishes a legal basis for the

28. Article 1(1), No. 54 Resolution of the Government of Georgia, 23 Jan. 2020 'On the Establishment of the Climate Change Council'.
29. Article 7, Governance Charter of the Climate Change Council.
30. No. 5646-RS The Law of Georgia on Energy and Water Supply, 20 Dec. 2019.
31. Article 1(2), No. 5646-RS The Law of Georgia on Energy and Water Supply, 20 Dec. 2019.
32. Article 1(3), *ibid.*

promotion, facilitation and use of energy from renewable sources. It also lays down provisions relating to support schemes, statistical transfers and joint projects between Georgia and EnC Contracting Parties (CPs), as well as with third countries, guarantees of origin, administrative procedures, provision of information and training, access to the electricity grid for energy from renewable sources. The law also establishes sustainability criteria for biofuels and bioliquids.[33]

36. The 2020 'Law of Georgia on Energy Efficiency' is a framework energy efficiency legislative act, which aims to reduce energy intensity, secure energy supply, increase energy independence and support other activities increasing energy efficiency. The aim of the 2020 'Law on Energy Performance of Buildings' is to promote reasonable usage of energy efficiency of buildings. The provisions of the law apply to almost all types of buildings ranging from individual houses to multistorey and residential buildings. This also includes the promotion of energy efficiency in the building sector: adequate implementation of the national legislation based on the energy performance of buildings directive, long-term building renovation strategies and achievement of nearly zero-energy and emission standards in buildings.[34]

37. Apart from these primary laws' setup, the national energy law system covers the 1999 'Law of Georgia on Oil and Gas' and a number of other secondary laws and acts enacted by the Parliament of Georgia (including the Country's state energy policy approval), GoG (e.g., market design concept), Ministry of Economy and Sustainable Development (e.g., security of supply rules) and GNERC.

38. ENP and EaP political forums are examples of soft law instruments that are not legally binding upon Georgia. The hard law instruments (e.g., EU-Georgia AA, which provides preferential access to EU markets, often with a view to eventual entrance to the EU customs union) in the EU external energy policy are different international treaties, to which the EU is a member and in which it tends to include its legal norms of consistently liberalized domestic legislation with the aim of expanding the area of factual application of the EU energy *acquis*. The EnC Treaty serves as another successful model of such hard law instrument for the states of South-Eastern Europe and beyond. As 'legally binding sectoral multilateralism',[35] EnC is a key pillar of the external dimension of the EU energy policy and a principal tool for modernizing Georgia's energy sector.[36]

39. The energy sector is a crucial aspect of the Association Agreement, underpinning an important part of EU-Georgia relations. Article 297 of the AA defines

33. No. 5652 Law of Georgia on Promoting the Production and Use of Energy from Renewable Sources, 20 Dec. 2019.
34. Article 6, No. 5898-SS Law of Georgia on Energy Efficiency, 21 May 2020.
35. S. Blockmans & V.B. Vooren, *Revitalizing the European Neighborhood Economic Community: The Case for Legally Binding Sectoral Multilateralism*, Working Paper, Leuven Centre for Global Governance Studies, 91 (2012).
36. For analysing nexus between human rights and energy, *see* Quintavalla, Alberto, Franz Kienzl, and Irakli Samkharadze. 'The human right to energy: drawing lessons from the development of the human right to water'. Journal of Human Rights and the Environment 14.1 (2023): 49–66.

the general cooperation principles between the EU and Georgia, based on the principles of partnership, mutual interest, transparency and predictability. This reflects the EU's endeavour to support the modernization of Georgia's energy legislation by offering convergence with its rules. Annex XXV of the AA specifies the concrete EU legal acts (regulations and directives) that need to be implemented in the fields of electricity, natural gas, oil, renewable energy and energy efficiency. In this respect, the AA details the implementation agenda and provides the timeline in which the domestic legislation should be approximated.

§4. The Energy Community

40. On 1 July 2017, Georgia acceded to the EnC Treaty ensuring closer bonds with the EU's energy market. Through this accession, the country becomes entitled to all rights granted to the CPs and subject to the obligations imposed on participatory states. Georgia's accession to the Treaty is regulated by the Protocol Concerning the Accession of Georgia to the Treaty Establishing the Energy Community (Accession Protocol – EnCT). In its legal nature, the Protocol is an international treaty binding on Georgia, which enjoys supremacy vis-à-vis conflicting national laws as long as it does not contradict the Constitution and the Constitutional Law of Georgia. According to Article 7 of the Law of Georgia on 'Normative Acts' and Article 6 of the Law of Georgia on 'International Treaties', the Protocol becomes an inherent part of the Georgian legal system as duly ratified by the Parliament of Georgia on 21 April 2017. For the purpose of compliance with Title II of the Treaty establishing the EnC and its related annexes, Article 2 of the Accession Protocol lists the number of EU legal acts to be aligned by Georgia. It provides a timeframe for the implementation of key reforms in the energy sector in the areas of electricity, gas, energy efficiency, renewable energy and energy-related environment.

41. Georgia's existing energy sector's primary and secondary legislation framework incorporates some aspects of regulation in accordance with EU principles. However, complying with EnC requirements obliges Georgia to change its energy legislation significantly and to create a new market framework, which will maintain to achieve security of supply, competitiveness and sustainability goals. In some cases, Georgia is able to request for derogations of specific issues for a certain period of time. Namely, according to Article 2(5) of the Accession Protocol, the South Caucasus Pipeline[37] and the North-South Gas Pipeline[38] are exempted from the implementation of Directive 2009/73/EC and Regulation (EC) No. 715/2009 until 31 August 2026, the date of expiration of the EnC Treaty. This will allow the country to implement EU Energy *acquis* sequentially while not harming public and private energy interests.

37. The South Caucasus Pipeline means SCP Project within the meaning ascribed to this term in the Intergovernmental Agreement between Georgia and the Azerbaijan Republic.
38. The North-South Gas Pipeline is a part of the Georgian Main Gas Pipelines System consisting of 1,200/1,000 mm diameter gas pipeline sections (as may be renewed, repaired, modified, refurbished, reconstructed and/or replaced) primarily assigned for transportation of natural gas from Russian Federation to the Republic of Armenia.

42. The accession of Georgia to the EnC Treaty can be considered as an 'endorsement' of already-assumed legal obligations under the AA and the obvious manifestation of a reliable energy partnership with the EU. Nevertheless, adopting the EU energy package in a timely manner brings significant uncertainty. This is reinforced by the fact that enforcement is the weakest feature of the Treaty. The EnC does not operate a supranational surveillance authority should Georgia not deliver on promises in due course. Specifically, compliance monitoring is conducted by the EnC Secretariat, which may initiate infringement procedures after having discovered or having been notified of Treaty violations. In practice, EnC enforcement is of a political nature, and the Secretariat will likely resort to diplomatic channels to encourage Georgia to adopt the EnC laws instead of opening infringement cases against Georgia for non-adoption of EnC rules.

Part I. Regulatory Framework Concerning Electricity

Chapter 1. Introduction

§1. Scope of the Law of Georgia on Energy and Water Supply

43. As mentioned above, accession to the EnC Treaty has become the initial point of reforms of the regulatory framework for the energy sector in Georgia. By signing the Protocol Concerning the Accession of Georgia to the EnCT on 14 October 2016, Georgia reaffirmed its obligation to fulfil the defined energy sector objectives under both the Association Agreement and the EnC Treaty. Henceforth, stable energy cooperation with the European Community has been strengthened.

44. By adopting the new Law of Georgia on Energy and Water Supply in December 2019, Georgia established a general legal framework for the generation, transmission, distribution, supply of and trade in electricity, with a view to the facilitated emergence, opening, development and integration of well-functioning, transparent and competitive electricity market. The law settles the rules relating to the governing, organizing, regulating, monitoring, and supervising cross-border exchanges in electricity, the criteria and procedures applicable to calls for tenders and the granting of authorizations for energy activities, operation of and access to electricity systems, public service obligations in the electricity sector, and the rights of customers and their protection.[39]

45. Establishing frameworks, within which security of supply policies are being defined, responsibilities of market participants are set, and procedures to safeguard security of supply are determined in compliance with the requirements of the competitive electricity market, primarily serve the purpose of implementing the '*Acquis Communautaire*'.[40]

39. Article 5(1), No. 5646-RS The Law of Georgia on Energy and Water Supply, 20 Dec. 2019.
40. '*Acquis Communautaire*' refers to the body of common rights and obligations which bind all the Member States together within the European Union. It is constantly evolving and comprises not only EU primary, secondary binding and non-binding legislation but also the Court of Justice of the European Union case law. More succinctly, it is a legal jargon to refer to the EU's supranational legal and regulatory regime.

46. In addition to these purposes, the law stipulates the main objectives in an extensive and comprehensive manner. It (a) establishes a legal framework for uninterrupted supply of electricity at defined quality standards for the benefit of all categories of customers in Georgia;[41] (b) ensures secure, reliable and efficient operation of electricity and natural gas systems, and the provision of related services to all system users;[42] (c) defines the rights and obligations of regulated undertakings and sets the rights and obligations of the GNERC, as well as establishes a legal framework for mutual relations among regulated undertakings and their relations with the Commission and other state authorities;[43] (d) creates conditions for a full opening of electricity and natural gas markets in Georgia based on the principles of competitiveness, transparency and non-discrimination aiming at unrestricted trade in electricity;[44] (e) establishes common rules for the organization and functioning of electricity market in Georgia, including its further development and, subject to future interconnections with EnC Parties, its pan-European integration;[45] (f) sets the terms and conditions for the provision of public service obligations in electricity sector, and ensures the protection of final customers;[46] (g) regulates and monitors the unbundling of Transmission System Operators (TSOs) and Distribution System Operators (DSOs), as well as ensures their effective independence from other energy activities and related commercial interests;[47] (h) creates adequate conditions for investments in electricity system, including interconnections with neighbouring systems, and in other facilities enhancing the security of supply;[48] (i) establishes a legal framework for regional and international cooperation of system and market operators, the Commission and other state authorities, as well as for mutual cooperation among competent national authorities, institutions and other public bodies of Georgia.[49]

47. Even back in 2015, the Parliament of Georgia adopted a resolution, 'Main Directions of the State Policy in Energy Sector of Georgia', which has become a long-term comprehensive state vision, with the core purpose to contribute to the future energy sector improvement. Roughly five years later, the new energy law served as a tool for the adoption of the new national strategy called 'The Energy Strategy of Georgia 2020–2030' which foresees further improvements and recommendations regarding ongoing energy sector reform. Furthermore, adopting a follow-up supportive resolution of the GoG, No. 246 'The Concept for the Georgian Electricity Market' made it even easier to establish a well-organized, cohesive electricity market structure by considering the objectives indicated in the Law of Georgia on Energy and Water Supply.[50]

---

41. Article 2(a), No. 5646-RS The Law of Georgia on Energy and Water Supply, 20 Dec. 2019.
42. Article 2(b), *ibid.*
43. Article 2(c), *ibid.*
44. Article 2(d), *ibid.*
45. Article 2(e), *ibid.*
46. Article 2(f), *ibid.*
47. Article 2(g), *ibid.*
48. Article 2(h), *ibid.*
49. Article 2(i), *ibid.*
50. Article 123(3), *ibid.*

48. The Concept for the Georgian Electricity Market establishes the guidelines for the organization and operation of the wholesale electricity market in Georgia, which aims to: (a) establish a model of the electricity market that ensures the creation of an attractive investment environment and the possibility of free choice for consumers, through the development of transparent and competitive markets, at both the wholesale and retail levels;[51] (b) establish an organized electricity market, including day-ahead, day-to-day, balancing and ancillary services, as well as establishing a market of bilateral agreements;[52] (c) separate rights and responsibilities among market subjects and redistribution of functions;[53] (d) format liquidity and competitive price in organized electricity markets, as well as the introduction of financial mechanisms necessary for the efficient and sustainable functioning of the market;[54] (e) facilitate the introduction of support mechanisms (scheme) provided by the Law of Georgia on Encouragement of Production and Use of Energy from Renewable Sources;[55] (f) determine the measures to be taken to move to the target model;[56] (g) fulfil the obligations under the Protocol on the Accession of Georgia to the Treaty establishing the Energy Union.[57]

49. It should be emphasized that competent Institutions Governing Activities set by the Law on Energy and Water Supply are: the Parliament of Georgia, the Government, the Ministry of Economy and Sustainable Development and the GNERC. Invoking Articles 6 and 7 of the Law of Georgia on Energy and Water Supply, other public bodies shall be responsible for taking relevant decisions with regard to the governing of energy activities too, within the scope of their specific competencies as assigned in accordance with the energy law, other applicable laws and their implementing regulations.

50. Apart from the linking functions between the Government, the Parliament and MoESD carrying out their standardized duties and responsibilities, it is vital to draw attention to the functions of the Commission.

§2. Georgian National Energy and Water Supply Regulatory Commission

51. For the purposes of this monograph, all provisions on the Commission will not be reviewed closely. The clauses described in this section display the most relevant functions of the Commission covering the regulation concerning electricity.

51. Article 1(1)(a), No. 246 Resolution of the Government of Georgia, 'The Concept for the Georgian Electricity Market'.
52. Article 1(1)(b), *ibid.*
53. Article 1(1)(c), *ibid.*
54. Article 1(1)(d), *ibid.*
55. Article 1(1)(e), *ibid.*
56. Article 1(1)(f), *ibid.*
57. Article 1(1)(g), *ibid.*

52. The Commission is a specialized, independent, autonomous and non-profit institution with the status of a legal person incorporated under the laws of Georgia, and the key energy activities are regulated, monitored and supervised by the Commission, which acts as a single national regulatory authority for energy in Georgia.[58]

53. When it comes to the objectives, the Commission takes all reasonable measures to promote, in close cooperation with the EnC Regulatory Board, regulatory authorities of other EnC Parties and the EnC Secretariat, competitive, secure and environmentally sustainable internal energy markets within the EnC, and effective market opening for all customers and suppliers in the EnC. The Commission ensures appropriate conditions for the effective and reliable operation of energy networks, taking into account long-term objectives.[59] It further develops the competitive and proper functioning of regional energy markets within the EnC[60] and eliminates restrictions on trade in energy between the EnC Parties, including developing appropriate cross-border transmission capacities to meet the demand and enhancing the integration of national markets which may facilitate energy flows across the EnC.[61]

54. In addition to the above, the Commission:

- helps to achieve, in the most effective way, the development of secure, reliable and efficient non-discriminatory systems that are customer-oriented, and promote system adequacy and, in line with general energy policy objectives, energy efficiency;[62]
- helps to achieve the integration of large- and small-scale generation of electricity from RES, and distributed production in both transmission and distribution networks;[63]
- facilitates access to the network for new capacities of the generation of electricity, in particular, removing barriers that could prevent access for new market entrants and of electricity from RES;[64]
- ensures that system operators and system users are granted appropriate incentives, in both short and long term, to increase efficiencies in system performance and foster market integration;[65]
- ensures that customers benefit through the efficient functioning of energy markets, promoting effective competition and helping to ensure customer protection;[66]

58. Article 18, No. 5646-RS The Law of Georgia on Energy and Water Supply, 20 Dec. 2019.
59. Article 28(1)(a), *ibid.*
60. Article 28(1)(b), *ibid.*
61. Article 28(1)(c), *ibid.*
62. Article 28(1)(d), *ibid.*
63. Article 28(1)(e), *ibid.*
64. Article 28(1)(f), *ibid.*
65. Article 28(1)(g), *ibid.*
66. Article 28(1)(h), *ibid.*

- helps to achieve high standards of public services provided in the electricity sector, contributing to the protection of vulnerable customers and contributing to the compatibility of necessary data exchange processes for switching supplier.[67]

55. The duties and powers of the Commission are comprehensively and substantially presented in the Law of Georgia on Energy and Water Supply, covering all the possible areas of the new Georgian Energy Framework. The Commission issues, modifies and revocates licences;[68] certificates TSOs and monitors their continued compliance with the requirements for independence and unbundling imposed on TSOs;[69] establishes the terms and conditions for the provision of services by regulated undertakings.[70] Further, it approves special regulatory requirements for accounting in regulated undertakings;[71] monitors and enforces their proper implementation;[72] establishes the terms and conditions regulating the provision of information possessed by regulated undertakings to system users and/or customers.[73]

56. The Commission aspires to create a properly functioning energy market by monitoring the performance of regulated undertakings and ensuring their compliance with respective obligations and requirements.[74] Moreover, it monitors the provision of public services and implementation of public service obligations and[75] keeps the registry of energy undertakings engaged in energy activities.[76]

57. It is equally important that the Commission adopts methodologies used for calculating and setting tariffs for the transmission and distribution of electricity,[77] sets fees for connection to the electricity distribution network[78] and for the services provided by the market operator.[79] The Commission adopts the methodology used for calculating allowable losses in electricity networks,[80] as well as the investment appraisal methodologies and ensures that methodologies adopted by the Commission are published sufficiently in advance within the reasonable time period prior to their entry into force.[81]

58. Assuredly, tariffs and fees shall be justified, reasonable, verifiable, nondiscriminatory, based on objective criteria, and determined in a transparent manner.

67. Article 28(1)(i), *ibid.*
68. Article 29(1)(a), *ibid.*
69. Article 29(1)(b), *ibid.*
70. Article 29(1)(c), *ibid.*
71. Article 29(1)(e), *ibid.*
72. Article 29(1)(f), *ibid.*
73. Article 29(1)(g), *ibid.*
74. Article 29(1)(h), *ibid.*
75. Article 29(1)(i), *ibid.*
76. Article 29(1)(j), *ibid.*
77. Article 29(1)(b)(a), *ibid.*
78. Article 29(1)(b)(b), *ibid.*
79. Article 29(1)(b)(c), *ibid.*
80. Article 29(1)(c), *ibid.*
81. Article 29(1)(e), *ibid.*

The Commission has the authority to supervise and monitor the following:

(a) The application of tariffs and fees and of respective methodologies, as well as enforcing their proper implementation.[82]
(b) Investment plans of system operators in charge.[83]
(c) Activities of TSO.[84]
(d) Compliance with and reviews of the past performance of network security and reliability rules.[85]
(e) The time taken by transmission and DSOs to make connections and repairs.[86]
(f) The implementation of safeguard measures in energy activities.[87]
(g) The level and effectiveness in the opening of energy markets and competition in energy markets.[88]
(h) The level of transparency in energy markets, including wholesale and retail prices.[89]
(i) The occurrence of restrictive contractual practices in energy markets.[90]
(j) Enforcement of conditions related to cross-border exchanges.[91]
(k) The quality and availability of technical and commercial data.[92]
(l) Congestion management of the electricity system, including interconnectors with neighbouring systems, and implementation of the congestion management rules.[93]
(m) The compliance of the transmission system owner and of the independent system operator with their obligations and issuance of penalties for non-compliance.[94]
(n) The relations and communication between the independent system operator and the transmission system owner.[95]
(o) Continuing compliance of the TSO with the requirements for its independence and unbundling.[96]

59. The Commission ensures that the customer protection measures are effective and enforced, so as to ensure:

82. Article 29(1)(g), *ibid.*
83. Article 29(1)(h)(d), *ibid.*
84. Article 29(1)(h)(e), *ibid.*
85. Article 29(1)(h)(g), *ibid.*
86. Article 29(1)(h)(h), *ibid.*
87. Article 29(1)(h)(k), *ibid.*
88. Article 29(1)(i)(b), *ibid.*
89. Article 29(1)(i)(c), *ibid.*
90. Article 29(1)(i)(f), *ibid.*
91. Article 29(1)(j)(a), *ibid.*
92. Article 29(1)(j)(b), *ibid.*
93. Article 29(1)(j)(c), *ibid.*
94. Article 31(1)(a), *ibid.*
95. Article 31(1)(b), *ibid.*
96. Article 49(1), *ibid.*

(a) fair and non-discriminatory treatment;[97]
(b) receipt of high-quality services;[98] and
(c) competition and prevention of anti-competitive actions.[99]

60. The Commission issues binding decisions and imposes effective, proportionate and dissuasive penalties on regulated undertakings not complying with their obligations.[100]

97. Article 29(1)(k)(a), *ibid.*
98. Article 29(1)(k)(b), *ibid.*
99. Article 29(1)(k)(c), *ibid.*
100. Article 29(1)(g), *ibid.*

Chapter 2. Participants in the Electricity Market

§1. Energy Entities

61. In terms of electricity generation in Georgia, there is an abundance of competitors (state-owned: Enguri HPP & Vardnili HPP; Georgian Industrial Group; Energo-Pro Georgia (EPG); Georgian Oil and Gas Corporation (GOGC); Georgian Global Utilities; Telasi; Georgian American Alloys (GAA); Peri), whereas, retail customers are supplied with electricity by two distribution companies (JSC Telasi, JSC EPG), hence they do not have the opportunity to freely change the supplier in a market that is independent of the interests of the network. JSC Telasi and JSC EPG own a distribution network, processing facilities and are suppliers at the same time; therefore, they are considered vertically integrated electricity undertakings. The framework energy law sets out the unbundling rules which will eventually eliminate this problematic matter ('duo' of Telasi and Energo- Pro Georgia), in the near future, which, in terms of market price regulation, will be of great help to the sector.

§2. Energy Customers

62. The law distinguishes six types of customers, especially: (1) eligible customer who is free to purchase electricity and/or natural gas from the supplier or trader of their choice; (2) final customer who purchases electricity and/or natural gas for their own use; (3) household customer who purchases electricity and/or natural gas for their own household consumption, excluding commercial or professional activities; (4) large customer defined as final non-household customer, the legal status of whom shall be defined by the Commission; (5) non-household customer who purchases electricity and/or natural gas which is not for their own household use, including producers and traders; (6) vulnerable customer is a household customer who due to their social status and/or health condition and in accordance with applicable legal acts is recognized by the competent national authority of Georgia as being a vulnerable customer to whom the right to system use and/or supply of electricity or natural gas is granted under special conditions.

Chapter 3. Electricity Generation

63. There are two main sources of electricity generation in Georgia: hydropower plants, which are the biggest source of electricity and thermal power plants, perceived as a guaranteed source of power, as a reliable supply. Lastly, wind power is also generated in Georgia, which is a relatively new type of source of electricity generation in the country (total 33 PP with capacity (Mega Watt (MW)) 4,257.12).[101]

64. Every cycle of electricity generation procedure in Georgia is governed by the Commission, hence the electricity undertaking which operates an electricity generating facility (power plant) needs to hold an authorization, a licence issued by the Commission in order to: (a) produce electricity in a facility (or facilities) commissioned for the operation and use of energy sources specified in a licence; (b) enter into contracts for sale and purchase of electricity; (c) enter into contracts for the provision of balancing and ancillary services and (d) access electricity transmission and/or distribution systems.[102]

65. However, in case of (a) micro-generating power plant electricity generation; (b) or if the electricity generation activities performed by a facility during its commissioning stage; (c) the electricity generated exclusively for personal (whether it is household or commercial) consumption by a producer, the electricity generation facilities that are not connected to the electricity transmission or distribution networks, undertakings can still engage in a respective energy activity without any prior consent or authorization.[103]

66. Licence applicants should provide the Commission with all the relevant documentation in order to ensure and justify their compliance with reformed market standards. Failure to prove their proper implementation may result in refusal by the Commission to issue a licence. Applicants shall ensure technical, economic, financial and operational (human resources) capability to perform functions particular to each respective licensed energy activity. They should also prove their ability to implement the measures required to ensure the quality of the services provided to market participants. It is equally essential to prove and ensure the ability to provide public services and implement applicable public service obligations. Along with all of that, a licence applicant shall submit to the Commission the following documents together with the licence application:

– documents proving the ownership or other form of legal possession of an electricity facility necessary to perform a particular energy activity. Where

101. Electricity Market Operator, Generation Licensees https://esco.ge/en/kvalifitsiuri-satsarmoebi/generation-licensees, accessed on 11 Sep. 2020.
102. Article 33, No. 5646-RS The Law of Georgia on Energy and Water Supply, 20 Dec. 2019.
103. Article 11(3), *ibid.*

relevant, the form of legal possession shall extend for the minimum period of time to be defined by the Commission;[104]

- approval for the commissioning of electricity;[105]
- documents proving the ownership or other form of legal possession of equipment necessary to perform a particular energy activity and to provide related services to market participants or, as the case may be, documents proving the outsourcing of such equipment and/or related operational or maintenance services;[106]
- layout of electricity network owned or otherwise legally possessed by the energy undertaking, where applicable, to be submitted in a form defined by the Commission;[107]
- technical conditions for the connection to the electricity network;[108]
- environmental impact assessment (EIA) report, in cases, where such a report is mandatorily required by applicable laws for a particular energy activity;[109]
- list of fixed assets and the audit report of a licence applicant; and[110]
- management and staff scheme (organizational structure) of a licence applicant proving that all professional functions related to a particular energy activity are covered by human resources of a licence applicant or, as the case may be, documents proving the outsourcing of respective professional functions.[111]

67. Licences shall be issued for an indefinite period of time, but the Commission enjoys the privilege to modify or revoke a licence when needed. Mainly, GNERC shall perform the supervision and, where appropriate, require individual electricity producers and other electricity undertakings to implement specific measures aimed at ensuring application of fair competition principles.

68. Upon granting a licence, the energy producer shall: comply with the requirements and under the specific terms of a licence for the generation of electricity, comply with the prescribed requirements pertaining to energy efficiency and environmental protection, maintain electricity generation facilities in proper working order, prepare and publish in the appropriate form a programme of measures for improvement of energy efficiency, and shall produce and publish in the appropriate form an annual report on the results of such measures, etc. Licence applicant is entitled to appeal any decision announced by the Commission.

---

104. Article 13(2)(a), *ibid.*
105. Article 13(2)(b), *ibid.*
106. Article 13(2)(c), *ibid.*
107. Article 13(2)(d), *ibid.*
108. Article 13(2)(e), *ibid.*
109. Article 13(2)(f), *ibid.*
110. Article 13(2)(g), *ibid.*
111. Article 13(2)(h), *ibid.*

Chapter 4. Electricity Transmission

69. Transmission is an activity of public interest, which encompasses the transport of electricity on the transmission network as well as the operation, maintenance and development under economic conditions of the transmission network, and other related activities necessary for secure, reliable and efficient functioning of the electricity system of Georgia.

70. Transmission is carried out by the TSO, designated by the Commission via issuance of a licence for the transmission. The TSO shall be organized as a specialized and independent energy undertaking with the status of a legal person. While carrying out its duties and fulfilling its tasks, the TSO shall be independent of any other energy activities, namely production, distribution, supply, trade and purchase of electricity and related commercial interests.[112]

71. One of the most important reforms that the new regulatory framework encompasses is the notion of unbundling.[113] Ownership Unbundling (OU) model for each TSO, including the action plan for its implementation, shall be decided by the Government as submitted by the Commission and in consultation with the EnC Secretariat. The Commission shall monitor the continuing compliance of the TSO with the requirements for its independence and unbundling.

72. In order to manage the transmission process and maintain high efficiency, each TSO shall be required to: (a) adopt annual plans for the transmission system development for a minimum period of ten years;[114] (b) implement transparent and efficient procedures as well as terms and conditions for non-discriminatory and unrestricted TPA to the transmission system;[115] (c) implement transparent and efficient procedures as well as terms and conditions for non-discriminatory and most viable connection of distribution systems and other energy facilities;[116] (d) implement the terms and conditions for and perform dispatching functions in the transmission system;[117] (e) implement the terms and conditions for and ensure balancing of the transmission system;[118] (f) implement the terms and conditions for and proceed with the procurement of ancillary services and provision of system services;[119] (g) implement the terms and conditions for and perform the functions of the capacity allocation and congestion management aiming at efficient use of the capacities in the transmission network, including interconnectors with other systems;[120] (h)

112. Article 42(3), No. 5646-RS The Law of Georgia on Energy and Water Supply, 20 Dec. 2019.
113. EU Directive 2009/72/EC.
114. Article 52(1)(b), *ibid.*
115. Article 52(1)(c), *ibid.*
116. Article 52(1)(d), *ibid.*
117. Article 52(1)(e), *ibid.*
118. Article 52(1)(f), *ibid.*
119. Article 52(1)(g), *ibid.*
120. Article 52(1)(h), *ibid.*

take appropriate safety measures for using the transmission system and other associated facilities;[121] (i) ensure the confidentiality of commercially sensitive information obtained from conducting business operations;[122] (j) collect and publish data and information necessary to meet the prescribed requirements related to transparency and monitoring of energy markets;[123] (k) contribute to security of supply through adequate transmission capacity and system reliability, and perform in compliance with the security of supply requirements;[124] (l) take measures to increase energy efficiency and ensure environmental protection;[125] (m) apply modern methods of the energy efficiency/demand-side management by observing minimal standards related to the maintenance and development of the transmission system, including interconnectors;[126] (n) cooperate and promote operational arrangements and the development of energy exchanges with other system operators and relevant interested parties in order to establish regional energy markets;[127] (o) set the minimum internal operational rules and obligations on network security in compliance with this law and transmission network code;[128] (p) facilitate the integration and liberalization of energy markets; (q) submit to the Commission and, where so required by law, to other competent national or international institutions the information and documents needed to enable them to exercises their duties;[129] (r) manage cross-border transmission of electricity through the transmission network under the conditions and in the manner established by those agreements and technical capacities of cross-border electricity transmission lines as well as of the overall electricity transmission network;[130] (s) manage cross-border transmission of electricity through the transmission network under the conditions and in the manner established by those agreements and technical capacities of cross-border electricity transmission lines as well as of the overall electricity transmission network, in line with international agreements which bind Georgia.[131] Producers, system operators and final customers, facilities of whom are connected to the transmission network shall, at the request of the TSO, deliver to the TSO data and information required for the purpose of system operation, management and development.

121. Article 52(1)(i), *ibid.*
122. Article 52(1)(j), *ibid.*
123. Article 52(1)(k), *ibid.*
124. Article 52(1)(l), *ibid.*
125. Article 52(1)(m), *ibid.*
126. Article 52(1)(n), *ibid.*
127. Article 52(1)(o), *ibid.*
128. Article 52(1)(p), *ibid.*
129. Article 52(1)(r), *ibid.*
130. Article 61(1), *ibid.*
131. Article 61(2), *ibid.*

Chapter 5. Electricity Distribution

73. Distribution is an activity of public interest which encompasses the transport of electricity on the distribution network, ensuring secure and reliable deliveries of electricity or natural gas for final consumption, as well as the operation, maintenance and development under economic conditions of the distribution network. The network itself is composed of electricity facilities, transformers, and medium-voltage and low-voltage lines of the voltage level (0,4-3,3-6-10-35-110 kV) not higher than 110 kV leading up to points of delivery within the electricity distribution system, in addition to other facilities, telecommunication and IT equipment and other infrastructure required for the functioning of the network.

74. Distribution is carried out by the DSO and organized as a specialized and independent energy undertaking with the status of a legal person, independent from any other energy activities, namely production, transmission, supply and trade, purchase and related commercial interests. Independence of the DSO shall be implemented and ensured through unbundling of the DSO.

75. DSOs shall be responsible for ensuring the long-term ability of the distribution system in their service area to meet reasonable demands for the distribution of electricity and for operating, maintaining and developing under economic conditions, a secure, reliable and efficient distribution system, with due regard for the environment and energy efficiency.[132] Distribution-related services shall be provided to individual system users on the basis of service contracts concluded with the DSO. Each DSO shall prepare and, subject to the approval of the Commission, adopt standard contracts on provision of its services, in particular on connection to the distribution network and on distribution services. Adopted standard contracts shall be published on the website of the DSO.[133]

76. DSOs shall not discriminate between system users or different categories of system users, particularly in favour of their related undertakings.[134] They are also bound to provide any other system operator, including transmission and DSOs, with sufficient information to ensure that the transport of electricity is in a manner compatible with the secure and efficient operation of interconnected systems.[135]

77. Unequivocally, DSOs must provide system users with detailed information in a meaningful, quantifiably clear and easily accessible way regarding services offered as well as conditions for such services and technical information necessary for system users to gain effective access to the system in consistency with confidential information exemptions approved by the Commission.[136] Starting from procuring the energy they use for carrying out their functions according to the

132. Article 74(1), No. 5646-RS The Law of Georgia on Energy and Water Supply, 20 Dec. 2019.
133. Article 74(3), *ibid.*
134. Article 74(4), *ibid.*
135. Article 74(5), *ibid.*
136. Article 74(6), *ibid.*

transparent, non-discriminatory and market-based procedures,[137] DSOs should also carry out other duties and perform tasks assigned to their competence.[138]

78. The framework law also implies that each DSO shall establish a development and investment plan with a view to ensuring the security, reliability, regularity and quality of the supply in the distribution network.[139] Further, the DSO ensures the connection of electricity facilities to the distribution network[140] and provides system users with non-discriminatory and unrestricted access to the distribution system in line with the terms and conditions laid down in the applicable Distribution Network Code. Charges for access to the distribution system shall be based on tariffs set by the Commission as calculated under its adopted methodology.[141]

79. The Distribution Network Code shall be developed and adopted by the Commission. It consists of rules for the functioning of the electricity distribution system, which is more of a technical nature and defines operational prerequisites for safety of the distribution network, procedure, terms and conditions for granting TPA to the distribution system criteria for planning the operation and development of the distribution network, etc.

80. In accordance with the principle of greater transparency, the DSO is obliged to publish an annual report on its activities in the previous calendar year in the form and within the timeframe established by the Commission.

137. Article 74(7), *ibid.*
138. Article 74(8), *ibid.*
139. Article 75(1), *ibid.*
140. Article 79(1), *ibid.*
141. Article 78(1), *ibid.*

Chapter 6. Electricity Consumption

81. Creating a new competitive market within the reformed framework ensures that consumers receive high-quality service, hence the need to take certain measures is on the agenda to protect certain public interests. In the process of energy market liberalization, it has become possible to impose public service obligations and set regulated conditions for market activities by the Government to protect the interests of end consumers and energy security. The public service obligation may be imposed on operating electricity companies to ensure security, including supply security, supply continuity, proper quality and price, as well as environmental protection, including energy efficiency, energy production from RES, and climate protection. Furthermore, Georgian energy law calls on all market participants to ensure high-quality service performance and provide customers with guaranteed, high-quality end products and services. The monitoring function is performed by the Commission.

82. Final customers shall be protected in accordance with energy law; therefore, each final customer is entitled to possess all relevant data in relation to its electricity consumption and shall be able to, by explicit agreement and free of charge, give any registered supplier access to its metering data. The General Supply Conditions shall define a format for the data and a procedure for suppliers and final customers to have access to the data. No additional costs shall be charged to the final customer for that service.[142]

83. On top of that, in the event of technical or other disturbances in the delivery of electricity or natural gas, which are not caused by the facilities of the final customers, the final customer shall have the right to demand the removal of those disturbances within the shortest possible period of time.[143] In addition to the abovementioned, each eligible customer is entitled to a free choice of supplier and change of supplier. Large customers shall have the right to contract simultaneously with several suppliers.

84. Protecting vulnerable customers is the novelty recognized by framework energy law; therefore, the protection of vulnerable consumers should be implemented in the context of the state social policy. In order to protect vulnerable consumers, state and municipal authorities, in consultation with the Commission and other stakeholders, develop special programmes, measures, and benefits to help meet the demand and/or to increase access to electricity and natural gas and identify eligible beneficiaries of these programmes, events or benefits.[144]

85. Likewise, a special protective mechanism has been established regarding Last Alternative Delivery (Customers of the Last Resort), in the form of public services, with limited time and regulated conditions, to end consumers who, due to

142. Article 122(3), No. 5646-RS The Law of Georgia on Energy and Water Supply, 20 Dec. 2019.
143. Article 122(5), *ibid.*
144. Article 112, *ibid.*

certain circumstances, have not been able to choose or lose their electricity supplier.[145] The last alternative supplier of electricity selected by the GoG is based on an open tender procedure.[146] The last alternative supplier can deliver to the end customer within no more than three calendar months. If the end customer fails to enter a supply contract with the new supplier within the specified period, the relevant system operator shall terminate its supply of electricity.[147]

145. Article 113, *ibid.*
146. Article 110(1), *ibid.*
147. Article 110(10), *ibid.*

Part II. Regulatory Framework Concerning Gas

Chapter 1. Introduction

§1. Scope of the Law of Georgia on Energy and Water Supply

86. The main regulatory framework concerning performance of activities, institutions and entities governed by the gas law is to be found in the Law of Georgia on Energy and Water Supply (hereinafter 'the law' or 'framework energy law'), published on 20 December 2019. According to Article 170, it came into force (except Chapters XXXIII and XXXIV and Article 148 with respect of the licence holders of water supply) on the date of its publication. Worth mentioning that with the adoption of the framework energy law, the Law of Georgia on Electricity and Natural Gas[148] became void. Article 1(1) of the Law of Georgia on Energy and Water Supply stipulates that the transmission of gas, distribution of gas, supply of natural gas, storage of natural gas and wholesale of natural gas are governed by the legislation so as to facilitate emergence, opening, development and integration of well-functioning, transparent and competitive natural gas (alongside electricity) markets.[149]

87. It has to be emphasized that the Law of Georgia on Energy and Water Supply was adopted in compliance with relative EU Directives and Regulations, in particular with Directive 2009/72/EC concerning common rules for the internal market in electricity; Regulation (EC) No. 714/2009 on conditions for access to the network for cross-border exchanges in electricity; Directive 2005/89/EC concerning measures to safeguard security of electricity supply and infrastructure investment; Directive 2009/73/EC concerning common rules for the internal market in natural gas; Regulation (EC) No. 715/2009 on conditions for access to the natural gas transmission networks and respectively Council Directive 2004/67/EC of 26 April 2004 concerning measures to safeguard security of natural gas supply.

88. According to Article 1(6), the conditions set forth for natural gas, including liquefied natural gas, also apply to gas that has been produced from biogas and

148. Article 169, *ibid.*
149. Article 1(1), *ibid.*

biomass and to other types of gas, considering it as technically manageable to incorporate into the natural gas system and transport it safely.[150] Article 1(6) also refers to requirements for exploration of natural gas; however, it is fair to say that these requirements are not frequently applied in practice, as the vast majority (almost 100%) of available natural gas resources in Georgia is imported.[151] It is also to be mentioned that the Law of Georgia on Energy and Water Supply does not apply to natural gas exploration operations and to the realization of natural gas through filling stations.

89. Regarding the objectives of the Law of Georgia on Energy and Water Supply, Article 2(a) respectively states that the main objective of the law is to ensure an uninterrupted supply of natural gas and to guarantee the secure, reliable and efficient operation of natural gas systems (Article 2(b)).[152] Article 2 also points to the rights and obligations of regulated undertakings; conditions for a fully opened gas markets based on the principles of competitiveness, transparency, and non-discrimination; functioning natural gas markets in Georgia and future interconnections with EnC Parties; public service obligations in the natural gas sector; principle of unbundling; conditions for investments and regional and international cooperation.

§2. Institutions Competent for Regulation of Activities Governed by Gas Law

90. As it is indicated in Article 6(1) of the law, the responsibilities for taking relevant decisions with regard to governing energy activities within the scope of their specific competences are shared between the Government, the Ministry (MoESD) and other public bodies.[153] However, only the Commission shall be designated and shall act as a single national regulatory authority.

91. In order to harmonize regulatory and administrative practices in the electricity and natural gas sectors, competent national authorities of Georgia shall ensure close cooperation at different national and regional levels. The Ministry, predominantly, is responsible for developing and implementing, in close cooperation with the Government, the Commission and other respective parties, the State Energy Policy for a period of at least ten years. The State Energy Policy then shall be adopted by the Parliament.

92. The State Energy Policy should cover short-term, medium-term and long-term strategies and priorities of the electricity and gas sectors. The document should apply appropriate measures so as to guarantee security of electricity and natural gas

150. Article 1(6), *ibid.*
151. *Ibid.*
152. Article 2(a), *ibid.*
153. Article 6(1), *ibid.*

supplies. It is noteworthy that such measures should ensure the availability, accessibility and affordability of electricity and natural gas. With this point of view, a long-term balance between supply and demand is also important. Consequently, the policy should also ensure the diversification of primary energy sources. It has to facilitate the use of renewable energy and, in addition, should aim to increase the efficiency of energy activities. In terms of efficiency and effectiveness, protection of the environment from any negative impact of energy activities also needs to be covered. Thus, it is also important to protect the rights and interests of all relative parties in these activities. The policy shall also aim to promote and attract investments and thus, facilitate competitiveness, transparency, non-discrimination and legal certainty in energy activities. Scientific research and education in the field of energy are of immense importance, hence the policy needs to cover respective provisions as well. Finally, other relevant analyses, forecasts and recommendations are also to be addressed.

93. Despite the fact that the Ministry is not a national regulatory authority, it has, nevertheless, the right to make decisions regarding deregulation and partial deregulation. As mentioned above, the Commission shall be designated and shall act as a single national regulatory authority, and it is the Commission's first and foremost competence to govern mandatory authorization of energy activities.

94. Under Article 11(b) of the law, transmission of natural gas, distribution of natural gas, operation of Liquid Natural Gas facilities, operation of the facilities of liquidated natural gas and the operation of natural gas market fall within energy activities that shall be subject to a prior licence to operate as issued by the Commission under the terms and conditions stipulated in the Law of Georgia on Licenses and Permits and in the Law of Georgia on Energy and Water Supply.[154] Article 11(2) stipulates that the above-mentioned energy activities without a valid licence issued by the Commission shall be forbidden.[155]

95. According to Article 12(1), the Commission shall issue licences only to undertaking, which complies with the requirements stipulated in the Law of Georgia on Licenses and Permits[156] and with specific licensing conditions stipulated in the law.[157] Article 13(1) refers to a procedure in accordance with which licences shall be issued. As indicated in the Law on Energy and Water Supply, licences shall be issued in a transparent, objective, legally justified and non-discriminatory manner in accordance with the procedures established by the Law of Georgia on Licenses and Permits.[158]

154. Article 11(b), *ibid.*
155. Article 11(2), *ibid.*
156. Article 12 (1), No. 1775 Law of Georgia on Licenses and Permits, 24 Jun. 2005.
157. Article 12(1), *ibid.*
158. Article 13(1), *ibid.*

96. In addition to the listed requirements established by the Law of Georgia on Licenses and Permits, a licence applicant in the field of energy activities shall submit to the Commission the documents that are to be found in Article 13(2). Licence applicants for transmission of electricity or natural gas shall be duly unhandled and certified. Unbundling is one of the main principles of modern energy law, and it has to be emphasized that in Georgia, it is still a challenge, as the state has only recently begun its reforms to incorporate relevant provisions in practice. In respect to Article 13(6), all licence holders are obliged to submit all the factual circumstances to the Commission upon its request, including respective documents, data and information, which prove meeting the terms of the licence conditions requested by the licence seekers. Issuance of the licence is certified with the licence certificate issued by the Commission in accordance with the Law of Georgia on Licenses and Permits.[159]

97. The licence seeker may be refused to be issued a licence only based on the Law of Georgia on Energy and Water Supply and the Law of Georgia on Licensing and Permits. The refusal to issue the licence should be justified legislatively and based on principles of objectivity, transparency and non-discrimination. The refusal should be defined respectively to the licence seeker.

98. The Law of Georgia on Energy and Water Supply provides an opportunity for a licence seeker to whom issuing the licence was refused to appeal the decision on the basis of the rule defined by the legislation of Georgia. Almost all cases of the refusal on issuing a licence on energy activities, together with its reasons, should be communicated to the EnC Secretariat.

159. Article 13(6), *ibid.*

Chapter 2. Natural Gas Market Participants

§1. Energy Entities

99. Entities operating in the natural gas market are the ones engaging in gas sector activities and energy customers. The energy entities recognized by gas legislation are GOGC JSC (state supplier), State Oil Company of Azerbaijan Republic (SOCAR) Georgia Gas LLC (retail/wholesale supplier), Tbilisi Energy LLC (retail/wholesale supplier), G.I Trading LLC (Retail/wholesale supplier) and other entities which are also retail/wholesale suppliers.

100. According to the Law of Georgia on Energy and Water Supply, Georgia has to choose the type of unbundling between OU and Independent System Operator.[160] Considering the fact that GOGC JSC resembles the model of an Independent System Operator, it will be easier to apply this type of model in practice.[161] Nevertheless, there are many steps ahead in order to accomplish effective unbundling:

- It is essential to guarantee the functional independence of the TSO (GOGC JSC).
- LLC Georgian Gas Transportation company shall not engage in energy activities relating to supply and trade of natural gas.
- Ten-year transmission network development plan, which was voluntarily prepared by GOGC JSC, shall be prepared and implemented in practice by TSO and the owner of the transmission system shall finance the investments that were agreed upon with the Commission.

101. In case the decision is taken in favour of the OU model,[162] GOGC JSC and LLC Georgian Gas Transportation company shall be supervised by two different state agencies. In addition, LLC Georgian Gas Transportation company shall not engage in energy activities relating to delivery and trade of natural gas. And, finally, the transmission network and all the infrastructure necessary for transmission system operation shall be owned by LC Georgian Gas Transportation company. Alternatively, quasi-OU is also an option which is to be found in European practice. In that practice, a vertically integrated company retains ownership of the transmission network; however, in such a capacity that would be equivalent to owners' rights.

102. The final decision regarding the two mentioned unbundling models is to be taken by the GoG. The suggested unbundling model and the implementation plan are proposed by the Commission in cooperation with EnC Secretariat.[163] With

---

160. T. Tsurtsumia & S. Janelidze, *Obligations in the Field of Energy Defined by the Protocol of Georgia's Accession to the Founding Agreement of the Energy Union* 31 (Konrad Adenauer Stiftung 2019).
161. *Ibid.*, 38.
162. *Ibid.*, 39.
163. *Ibid.*

respect to the law requirements regarding independence and unbundling of natural gas, TSOs shall be satisfied within twenty-one months from the date the law came into force.[164]

§2. Unbundling of Natural Gas Transmission Companies

103. EU 'Third Energy Package',[165] which was introduced in 2009, also mentions DSOs unbundling from delivery activities; however, in contrast with the certified TSOs, it is sufficient for them to be functionally and legally independent. According to the framework of energy law, the Ministry is competent to make exceptions regarding functional and legal independence for the type of vertically integrated companies that serve less than 100,000 customers. In case the Ministry applies the above-mentioned competence, unbundling provisions shall only be applied to the three largest DSOs that are at the same time engaged in natural gas supply activities – SOCAR Georgia Gas LLC, Tbilisi Energy LLC and JSC Sakorggas.[166]

§3. Energy Customers

104. Article 3(u) of the law defines 'customer' as the end user of electricity and/or natural gas or a trader, or an energy undertaking which purchases electricity and/or natural gas, user or drinking water.[167] The law makes a distinction between the 'eligible customer' and 'final customer/end user'. The 'eligible customer' shall mean an end user who is authorized to purchase electricity and/or natural gas from the supplier or trader of its choice or at the organized market in accordance with the rules of supply or market, while the 'final customer/end user' shall mean a customer/user purchasing electricity and/or natural gas for his own use.

105. The law also mentions 'large customer', 'non-household customer', 'protected customer' and 'vulnerable customer'. The 'large customer' shall mean a final non-household customer, the legal status of which shall be defined by the Commission, while 'non-household customer' shall mean a customer purchasing electricity and/or natural gas which is not for his own household use, including producers and traders.

106. 'Protected customer' shall mean household customers and small enterprises connected to a natural gas distribution network, and essential social services connected to a natural gas distribution or transmission network, as well as district

164. *Ibid.*
165. The European Commission, 21 May 2019. *Third Energy Package*: https://ec.europa.eu/energy/topics/markets-and-consumers/market-legislation/third-energy-package_en.
166. T. Tsurtsumia & S. Janelidze, *Obligations in the Field of Energy Defined by the Protocol of Georgia's Accession to the Founding Agreement of the Energy Union* 31 (Konrad Adenauer Stiftung 2019).
167. Article 3(u), No. 5646-RS The Law of Georgia on Energy and Water Supply, 20 Dec. 2019.

heating installations to the extent that they deliver heating to the above-mentioned customers, provided that these installations are not able to switch to other fuels and are connected to a natural gas distribution or transmission network.

107. 'Vulnerable customer' shall mean a household customer who due to their social status and/or health condition and in accordance with applicable legal acts is recognized by the competent national authority of Georgia as being a vulnerable customer to whom the right to system use and/or supply of electricity or natural gas is granted under special conditions in accordance with the provisions of the law.

Chapter 3. Natural Gas Production/Exploitation

108. In Georgia, gas production/exploitation is regulated under the Law of Georgia on Energy and Water Supply, the Law of Georgia on Oil and Gas and its implementing regulations.

109. Article 39(1) of the Law of Georgia on Energy and Water Supply stipulates that gas exploitation shall be produced by any business entity authorized for processing of natural gas in facilities commissioned and operating under the terms and conditions stipulated in the Law of Georgia on Oil and Gas and its implementing regulations.[168] Under paragraph 2, each natural gas producer, subject to its compliance to paragraph 1 of Article 39(1) of the Law of Georgia on Energy and Water Supply, shall be entitled to trade in natural gas on the natural gas market of Georgia, following its registration by the natural gas market operator as a natural gas market participant in accordance with the Natural Gas Market Rules. Articles 40 and 41 refer respectively to the rights and obligations of natural gas producers.

110. Namely, under Article 40, each natural gas producer has the right to: (1) enter into contracts for the sale and purchase of natural gas under the terms and conditions stipulated in the Law and the Natural Gas Market Rules; (2) enter into contracts for the provision of balancing and ancillary services under the terms and conditions stipulated in the Law, the Natural Gas Transmission Network Code and/or the Natural Gas Distribution Network Code and/or, when applicable following the establishment of the organized natural gas balancing and ancillary services markets, in the Natural Gas Market Rules; and (3) access natural gas transmission and/or distribution systems under conditions established by the law, the Natural Gas Transmission Network Code, the Natural Gas Distribution Network Code and other applicable legal acts.[169] Natural gas producers shall be entitled to other rights as well, provided by the Law of Georgia on Energy and Water Supply, other applicable laws and/or their implementing regulations.

111. As already mentioned above, Article 41 of the law sets the obligations for natural gas producers. Consequently, each natural gas producer shall be obliged to: (1) comply with the requirements and conditions laid down in the Law, the Natural Gas Market Rules and other applicable legal acts; (2) meet and comply with technical and operational rules specified in the Natural Gas Transmission Network Code and the Natural Gas Distribution Network Code; (3) comply with the prescribed requirements pertaining to energy efficiency and environmental protection; (4) place at the disposal of a transmission or DSO data and information required for the operation and management of the natural gas system; and (5) provide transmission and DSO with free access to the equipment in its natural gas production facilities which are being used for the delivery of natural gas to the transmission or distribution networks, respectively.[170] Article 41(2) of the Law of Georgia on Energy and

168. Article 39(1), *ibid.*
169. Article 40, *ibid.*
170. Article 41, *ibid.*

Water Supply refers to a situation when the GoG perceives the necessity to introduce additional requirements, so as to improve energy efficiency in natural gas production.[171]

112. Georgia does not possess satisfactory reserves of oil and gas (two main types of traditional resources) and, therefore, nearly 100% of natural gas and oil are imported from abroad. Therefore, it is extremely necessary for the state to strengthen and facilitate the work to search and rescue oil and gas resources on its territory. Considering the fact that natural gas alongside oil products and coal are the primary traditional energy sources in Georgia, the state heavily depends on international political atmosphere and which, by any means, questions the ability to ensure energy security for its citizens.

171. Article 41(2), *ibid.*

Chapter 4. Natural Gas Transportation

113. Transportation of imported and locally produced natural gas to the transmission network and final consumer through high voltage pipelines is undertaken by 'LLC Georgian Gas Transportation company' which is a state-owned licence holder entity of natural gas transportation.[172] 'LLC Georgian Gas Transportation company' is operating, through a lease, 'JSC GOGC's natural gas transportation system'. 'JSC GOGC's' 100% share is owned by the state through 'JSC Partnership Fund (PF)'.[173] Both the 'JSC GOGC' and 'LLC Georgian Gas Transportation company' are governed by the MoESD. Natural Gas Transportation System has seven points of receipt of which three are local points.

172. T. Tsurtsumia & S. Janelidze, *Obligations in the Field of Energy Defined by the Protocol of Georgia's Accession to the Founding Agreement of the Energy Union* 26 (Konrad Adenauer Stiftung 2019).
173. *Ibid.*

Chapter 5. Natural Gas Supply and Distribution

114. According to Article 80(1) of the law, distribution is an activity of public interest which encompasses the transport of electricity or natural gas on the distribution network, ensuring secure and reliable deliveries of electricity or natural gas for final consumption, as well as the operation, maintenance and development under economic conditions of the distribution network, and other related activities necessary for the efficient functioning and access to electricity and natural gas distribution systems of Georgia.[174] Distribution shall be carried out by the DSO under the terms and conditions stipulated in the law, as well as in line with other applicable laws and/or other legal acts regulating activities in the energy sector of Georgia.

115. The DSO shall be organized as a specialized and independent energy undertaking with the status of a legal person incorporated under the laws of Georgia. The DSO shall not be entitled to the sale and/or purchase of electricity or natural gas, except for in cases expressly referred to in the law. The DSO shall be designated by the Commission by issuance of a licence for the distribution under the terms and conditions stipulated in the Law of Georgia on Licenses and Permits in accordance with Chapter V of the Law of Georgia on Energy and Water Supply.

116. Where DSO is part of a vertically integrated undertaking, it shall be independent at least in terms of its legal form, organization and decision-making from other activities, not relating to distribution. Dissimilar to the electricity sector, in the natural gas sector, the law distinguishes distribution and supply activities; however, it is nevertheless, possible for the same undertaking to operate in both activities.

117. In 2018, the Commission issued twenty-six natural gas distribution licences.[175] The three largest licence holders – 'SOCAR Georgia Gas LLC', 'Tbilisi Energy LLC' and 'JSC Sakorggas' distributed 90% of the natural gas total capacity. The majority of distribution activity licence holders also engage in supply activities, and with regard to six licence holders, in 2018, the network was utilized by more than one supplier.[176] 'SOCAR LLC' with its enterprises is the main actor in both natural gas wholesale and retail markets and is the owner of the largest distribution network in Georgia.

118. In 2018, thirty-one supplier companies were operating in the natural gas retail market. The retail market is divided into 'social' and 'commercial' markets. The 'social segment' consists of the end customers (alongside Power Plants) who consume natural gas in an environment where tariffs are set by the Commission. It

174. Article 80(1), No. 5646-RS The Law of Georgia on Energy and Water Supply, 20 Dec. 2019.
175. T. Tsurtsumia & S. Janelidze, *Obligations in the Field of Energy Defined by the Protocol of Georgia's Accession to the Founding Agreement of the Energy Union* 28 (Konrad Adenauer Stiftung 2019).
176. *Ibid.*

is precisely the 'social segment' that benefit from 'cheap' gas, that the Government receives according to 'British Petroleum' contracts.[177]

119. As for the 'commercial segment', it consists of non-household customers and the type of household customers whose gasification process took place after 1 September 2007. Supply of natural gas is deregulated for 'commercial sector' and is set upon parties' agreement, on the basis of supplier's publicly proposed price.[178] Retail market, despite its partial deregulation, is characterized by high concentration, as the majority of its shares are owned by companies that hold dominant positions in the market. It has to be emphasized that despite the fact that formally consumers have the right to change supplier, there is no efficient stimulus to apply that provision in practice.

177. *Ibid.*
178. *Ibid.*

Chapter 6. Natural Gas Storage and Storage Management

120. According to the Law of Georgia on Energy and Water Supply, storage of natural gas shall be carried out by the natural gas storage system operator under the terms and conditions stipulated in the law, as well as in line with other applicable laws and/or other legal acts regulating activities in Georgia.[179] By means of the Law of Georgia on Licenses and Permits, in accordance with the terms defined by the rules of licensing approved by the law and the Commission, by means of issuing the licence of operating the natural gas storage system, authorizes the natural gas enterprise as the operator of the system of natural gas storage (which possesses the natural gas storage site) with the right of property and/or use. Licence for the storage of natural gas may be issued only to a duly unbundled natural gas storage system operator in accordance with Article 84 of the Law of Georgia on Energy and Water supply.[180]

121. Article 84 of the Law of Georgia on Energy and Water Supply refers to unbundling of natural gas storage system operator and states that natural gas storage system operator which is part of a vertically integrated undertaking shall be independent at least in terms of its legal form, organization and decision-making from other activities, not relating to transmission, distribution and/or storage.[181]

122. The following requirements shall apply in order to meet the criteria of independence by the natural gas storage system operator:

- Persons responsible for the management of the natural gas storage system operator shall not participate in company structures of the integrated natural gas undertaking responsible, directly or indirectly, for the day-to-day operation of the production and supply of natural gas.
- Appropriate measures shall be taken to ensure that the professional interests of persons responsible for the management of the natural gas storage system operator are taken into account in a manner that ensures that they are capable of acting independently.
- The natural gas storage system operator shall have effective decision-making rights independent from the integrated natural gas undertaking, with respect to assets necessary to operate, maintain or develop the storage facilities.
- The natural gas storage system operator shall establish a compliance programme, which sets out measures taken to ensure that discriminatory conduct is excluded and observance of it is adequately monitored.

179. *Ibid.*
180. Article 84, No. 5646-RS The Law of Georgia on Energy and Water Supply, 20 Dec. 2019.
181. *Ibid.*

Chapter 7. Gas Trade

123. According to the Law of Georgia on Energy and Water supply, Georgian energy law, among other things, regulates cross-border trade of electricity and natural gas. The trade itself, pursuant to the respective law, is defined as buying or selling electricity and/or natural gas on the territory of Georgia or for the purpose to resell it outside the state's borders. The law states that the trade of natural gas is considered to be an energy activity. Articles 28 and 29 set some more specific requirements for the Commission to regulate cross-border natural gas trade.

Chapter 8. Gas Consumption

124. As already mentioned above, 'customer' is an end user of electricity and/or natural gas or a trader, or an energy undertaking which purchases electricity and/or natural gas, user or drinking water. The law also mentions vulnerable customer as a household customer which due to their social status and/or health condition and in accordance with applicable legal acts is recognized by the competent national authority of Georgia as being vulnerable customer to whom the right to system use and/or supply of electricity or natural gas is granted under special conditions in accordance with the provisions of the framework energy law.

125. Concerning the quality of natural gas, it is indicated in the Law of Georgia on Energy and Water Supply that energy undertakings providing public services shall ensure prescribed or contracted quality of natural gas supplies. Public service obligation by itself shall mean a duty imposed upon an energy undertaking entrusted with the provision of services of general economic interest, which may relate to security, including security of supply, regularity, quality and price of supplies, and environmental protection. The duty of public service should be non-discriminative and not distort competition beyond what is strictly necessary in order to achieve the public service in question; Providing public services as an energy company in line with the law is not the same as exercising public legal authority defined by Georgia's administrative code. .

126. It is the Commission that sets the standards for natural gas supply requirements in order to guarantee high-quality natural gas supply for consumers. Article 110 of the Law of Georgia on Energy and Water Supply refers to 'Supply of last resort' and says that in case the customer loses electricity or natural gas supply without any form of protection, regardless of whether the concerned customer is faced with unplanned or planned exit of the supplier or a severe violation by the supplier of its obligations, the supplier of last resort shall supply a final customer with electricity or natural gas without a specific application having to be submitted.[182]

127. As for the final customers, they shall pay for electricity and natural gas in accordance with the General Supply Conditions and other applicable contractual conditions. Terms and procedures for invoicing, settlement and collections of payments shall be defined in the General Supply Conditions. In addition to this, each final customer is entitled to possess all relevant data in relation to its electricity and natural gas consumption and shall be able to, by explicit agreement and free of charge, give any registered supplier access to its metering data.

128. In the event of technical or other disturbances in the delivery of electricity or natural gas, the final customers shall have the right to demand the removal of

182. Article 110, *ibid.*

those disturbances within the shortest possible period of time under the terms and conditions of transmission or distribution network, if the mentioned disturbance is caused due to its facilities.

Part III. The Regulatory Framework Concerning Petrol

Chapter 1. Performance of Activities, Institutions and Entities Governed by the Petroleum Law

§1. Introduction

129. The Law of Georgia on Oil and Gas (hereinafter 'Petroleum Law') governs oil and gas prospecting, exploration and extraction activities as well as activities directly related to these operations, namely: collection, preparation, measurement and storage of the extracted oil and gas. It should be pointed out that the law uses the notion of 'Oil' as a synonym for 'Petroleum'. Pursuant to the Petroleum Law, oil is a complex of natural hydrocarbon compounds, under normal atmospheric pressure and temperature,[183] whereas the Petroleum products mean hydrocarbon mixtures obtained as a result of crude oil processing.[184]

130. In Georgia, the Petroleum Law aims to: (a) create a unified legal framework for the development of oil and gas resources and oil refining, gas processing or transportation activities and to pursue a unified national policy in the field of development of oil and gas resources and oil refining, gas processing or transportation activities in Georgia; (b) promote the attraction of investments in the field of oil and gas and protect legitimate interests of the entities involved in oil and gas operations in Georgia; (c) create an effective legal framework for state regulation, supervision and control of oil and gas operations, oil refining, gas processing and/or transportation activities in Georgia; (d) establish basic principles of oil and gas prospecting and exploration and extraction contracts between the state and an investor; (e) determine functions of the National Oil Company (NOC); (f) create a state regulatory body for oil and gas operations, oil refining, gas processing, and/or transportation activities in Georgia and determine its basic functions.[185]

131. Referring to the country's oil dependency matter, the share of imported petroleum products and natural gas in the structure of total primary energy

183. Article 1(1)(a), No. 1892 The Law of Georgia on Oil and Gas, 16 Apr. 1999.
184. Article 1(2)(f), *ibid.*
185. Article 3, *ibid.*

consumption of Georgia is about 65%–70%, which leads to the critical dependence of the country on expensive, imported hydrocarbons.[186]

§2. INSTITUTIONS COMPETENT FOR REGULATION OF ACTIVITIES GOVERNED BY THE OIL AND GAS LAW

132. The following institutions are competent for regulating the activities governed by the oil and gas law: GoG, represented by MoESD, the State Agency for Oil and Gas (hereinafter 'Agency' or 'SAOG') and the NOC.

133. SAOG is the legal entity under public law within MoESD. It carries out state regulation of oil and gas operations, oil refining, gas processing, and/or transportation activities. SAOG selects areas to be offered to investors to carry out oil and gas operations.[187] It establishes tender conditions and auction rules under which the winner to use the area offered to investors to carry out oil and gas operations shall be selected,[188] and thus SAOG arranges and conducts tenders and auctions and selects the winner.[189] Importantly, SAOG prepares all contracts, negotiates and signs contracts on behalf of the state;[190] issues licences to investors;[191] supervises and controls performance of the conditions and activities provided in a contract concluded under the law and a blanket licence for the use of oil and gas resources; provides investors with conditions necessary to perform duties under a contract and a blanket licence;[192] establishes and manages the central information base for all data and information related to the oil and gas resources and operations in Georgia;[193] takes into account market economy principles and the national interests; issues normative acts in order to create a non-discriminatory legal environment and effectively carry out oil and gas operations;[194] transfers all contractual operational and commercial duties (except for the regulatory functions) to the NOC for as long as the state of Georgia and/or a company with more than 50% equity participation of the state owns more than 50% of its shares; controls the performance of all contractual operational and commercial duties that were transferred to the NOC;[195] issues oil refining, natural gas processing, oil or natural gas transportation licences (business licences) on behalf of the state; issues all necessary permits and approves funds;[196] supervises and controls the performance of the conditions under a business licence and the oil refining, gas processing and transportation activities; provides business licence holders with the conditions necessary for them to perform

186. Chapter 4, The Energy Strategy of Georgia 2020–2030.
187. Article 8(1)(a), No. 1892 The Law of Georgia on Oil and Gas, 16 Apr. 1999.
188. Article 8(1)(b), *ibid.*
189. Article 8(1)(c), *ibid.*
190. Article 8(1)(d), *ibid.*
191. Article 8(1)(e), *ibid.*
192. Article 8(1)(f), *ibid.*
193. Article 8(1)(g), *ibid.*
194. Article 8(1)(h), *ibid.*
195. Article 8(1)(i), *ibid.*
196. Article 8(1)(k), *ibid.*

duties under the business licence;[197] supervises the oil refining and gas processing to ensure environmental safety and quality of oil and gas products;[198] if necessary, creates and manages a laboratory in compliance with the legislation of Georgia;[199] establishes and manages the central information base for all data and information related to oil refining, gas processing and transportation activities;[200] takes into account the national interests, policies and market economy principles; issues normative acts in order to effectively carry out oil refining, gas processing and transportation activities;[201] contributes to the development, modification and approval of the standards for raw materials and oil and gas products;[202] establishes tariffs for the transportation of raw materials and oil and gas products;[203] and approves the limits of natural losses occurring during oil and gas operations.[204]

134. The GoG has authorized the status of NOC with more than 50% of the shares owned by the state of Georgia. NOC shall perform the following activities: (a) participate in preparation of an oil and gas contract and in contract-related negotiations, initiate the contract before it is officially signed by the agency; (b) act as a commercial partner on behalf of Georgia when performing contracts; (c) dispose off a portion of the oil and gas extracted in Georgia that belongs to the state, pay the regulatory fee and transfer all the taxes imposed on it under a production-sharing contract to the state budget; (d) carry out state expertise of the mining operations plans and the process flow diagrams for the development of oil- and gas-containing subsoil; (e) if there is a production-sharing contract, jointly with the investor on a parity basis, set up a Coordinating Committee, the functions of which shall be defined as, but not limited to, the approval of work programmes, budgets and development plans and control over their implementation together with the agency; (f) perform all other functions that may be entrusted to it under the legislation of Georgia.[205]

135. NOC is also entitled to conclude a contract with a third party in its own name or through an affiliated company to participate in contracts under the Civil Code of Georgia together with other companies and institutions. Therefore, it shall be authorized to acquire, possess, sell or transfer its shares and to participate in cooperative and partnership agreements with third parties in Georgia and foreign states.[206]

---

197. Article 8(1)(l), *ibid.*
198. Article 8(1)(m), *ibid.*
199. Article 8(1)(n), *ibid.*
200. Article 8(1)(o), *ibid.*
201. Article 8(1)(p), *ibid.*
202. Article 8(1)(q), *ibid.*
203. Article 8(1)(r), *ibid.*
204. Article 8(1)(s), *ibid.*
205. Article 9(2), *ibid.*
206. Article 9(3), *ibid.*

§3. PARTICIPANTS IN THE PETROLEUM MARKET

I. Energy Entities

136. Oil and gas operations in Georgia are carried out by the following contractor companies: 'KBOC' (License Blocks: XIC, XID, XIE, XIF, XIII); 'Frontera Eastern Georgia' (License Block: XII); 'WGPEC' (License Block: V); 'GCE' Ltd (License Blocks: VIA, VIB); 'Schlumberger Rustaveli Company' (License Blocks: IX, X, XIB); 'Georgian Oil and Gas' (License Blocks: VIII, XIG, XIM, XIN, XIC Martkopi, XIC North Horseback Riding); 'Vectra Investment' (License Block: VIIB); 'Georgian Oil and Gas' Corporation (License Block: XIB); 'Block Energy' (License Block: XIF, XIC Norio-Satskhenisi, XIC Satskhenisi, Norio and Satskhenisi deposits up to 2,000 m deep).[207]

137. Primary petroleum product importers are: 'SOCAR Georgia', 'Lukoil Georgia', 'Wissol Petroleum', 'Rompetrol Georgia' and 'Gulf'. They control a significant segment of the country's oil market. Only two licensed oil refineries operate in the market, 'Globusi MB Ltd.' and 'ZD Oil Company Ltd.' with a capacity of 80,000 tons and 130,000 tons of crude oil per year, respectively.[208]

II. Energy Customers

138. The Petroleum Law does not define who the consumers are; however, the ultimate target of oil extraction and refining, supply, and distribution is always the one who ultimately consumes the product and is willing to invest material resources for the final product.[209] The main consumer of petroleum products in the country is the transport sector. The local oil market serves transit vehicles in the airspace of the country, as well as airports and seaports. Without any prior categorization, all customers enjoy the privilege to freely choose petroleum product suppliers in their preference.

207. Chapter 4, The Energy Strategy of Georgia 2020–2030.
208. *Ibid.*
209. Preamble (10), No. 242 The Law of Georgia on Subsoil, 17 May 1996.

Chapter 2. Petroleum Crude Production/Exploitation

139. Oil and gas operations may be performed by the state and natural or legal persons (hereinafter 'investor') on the basis of a contract concluded for the use of petroleum resources. Whether crude petroleum production/exploitation is considered energy activity or not, the process itself has a lot to do with adjacent areas, regarding authorization. SAOG issues blanket licences for the use of petroleum resources, upon application.[210]

140. Needless to say, the licence holder shall comply with each and every predetermined condition in order to successfully operate on the market. If a licence holder fails to execute a decision of the agency or violates the licence conditions, the agency shall consider and decide on the issue of terminating or revoking a licence. The maximum effective period of a contract and a respective licence shall be twenty-five years.[211] A contract may be extended on the initiative of an investor for a period necessary to economically and rationally extract, use and protect oil and gas.[212]

141. Pursuant to the Petroleum Law, the oil and gas resources existing in the subsoil within the territory of Georgia shall be owned by the state. Hence, the land ownership right does not include the right of ownership or exploitation of petroleum existing in the subsoil of the land. The right of ownership of extracted resources shall be determined in accordance with a contract.

142. In view of the foregoing, a production-sharing contract will be drawn up, whereby the rules and the procedure for sharing profits between an oil and gas investor and the state will be accurately determined. The state reserves the opportunity to receive royalties, and additional profits through this contract by imposing fees for the use of natural resources.

143. The right to explore and extract petroleum arises on the basis of winning a tender and/or auction, conducted solely by the agency.[213] A contract under which an investor is granted the rights to exploit and use resources shall be made between the state and the investor, characterized as a public-private partnership.

144. The law stipulates extensive provisions regarding any contract concluded between the agency and an investor, namely, conditions for reimbursement of expenses and product distribution,[214] procedure for determining the market price for oil and gas and the value of cost recovery oil,[215] the rights of ownership of the

210. Article 15^1, No. 1892 The Law of Georgia on Oil and Gas, 16 Apr. 1999.
211. Article 16(1), *ibid.*
212. Article 16(2), *ibid.*
213. Governed by No. 2273-IIS The Law of Georgia on Public-Private Partnerships, 4 May 2018.
214. Article 12(1)(c), No. 1892 The Law of Georgia on Oil and Gas, 16 Apr. 1999.
215. Article 12(1)(d), *ibid.*

extracted oil and gas,[216] the legal status, functions and duties of an operating company established to perform oil and gas operations,[217] the right of ownership of the property constructed and used for the extraction of oil and gas,[218] the rules and conditions for the use of common infrastructure facilities,[219] the controls for performing the contract conditions and the rights and duties granted under the licence,[220] conditions for performing liquidation work,[221] the insurance terms and conditions.[222]

145. In terms of protection control, a business licence holder shall, periodically, at least once a year, submit to the laboratory samples of raw materials or oil and gas products for testing.[223] Experts of the agency may periodically enter oil refining, gas processing and transportation activity areas, take samples of raw materials or oil and gas products and submit them to the laboratory for testing.[224] If the quality of raw materials or oil and gas products fails to comply with the established standards, the agency may issue an administrative legal act to terminate a business licence.[225]

216. Article 12(1)(e), *ibid.*
217. Article 12(1)(f), *ibid.*
218. Article 12(1)(p), *ibid.*
219. Article 12(1)(t), *ibid.*
220. Article 12(1)(u), *ibid.*
221. Article 12(1)(v), *ibid.*
222. Article 12(1)(w), *ibid.*
223. Article 25[11](2), No. 1892 The Law of Georgia on Oil and Gas, 16 Apr. 1999.
224. Article 25[11](3), *ibid.*
225. Article 25[11](4), *ibid.*

Chapter 3. Petroleum (Crude Oil and Petroleum Products) Pipeline Transportation

146. Entities are not limited in their choice of choosing means of transportation, since they can freely operate within their authorization limits. A blanket licence holder for oil and gas resources, its affiliated company or any other person may submit an application to the agency for a transportation licence only to transport products that are produced by it, or its raw materials or oil and gas products.[226]

147. For the aims of the law, regardless of the type of transportation, it must be available to all carriers on a non-discriminatory basis. Pipeline transportation is the most entrenched type of transportation, since the Baku-Tbilisi-Ceyhan pipeline and the Western Route Export Pipeline (WREP) pass through Georgia.

148. It should be pointed out that the investor may hold negotiations about the commercial use of free volumes of the state-owned trunk pipelines. After granting permission, an investor may build and use an oil and gas trunk pipeline to be connected to the existing trunk pipeline for exporting its contractual portion of oil and gas.[227] Unfortunately, the country has practically no oil refining capacity, even to partially meet its own needs. A part of the crude petroleum extracted in Georgia is exported through Batumi and Poti terminals, while a significant part is processed in local, small-capacity oil refineries.

226. Article 25^2, No. 1892 The Law of Georgia on Oil and Gas, 16 Apr. 1999.
227. Article 21(2), *ibid.*

Part IV. Regulatory Framework Concerning Energy Efficiency

Chapter 1. Scope of the Law of Georgia on Energy Efficiency

149. On 21 May 2020, Georgia adopted the Law on Energy Efficiency and the Law on Energy Efficiency of Buildings. The forerunner of the above-mentioned laws was the adoption of the Energy Labeling Law, which is directly related to the introduction of energy efficiency mechanisms, namely EU Energy Efficiency Directives (2012/27/EU, 2010/31/EU, 2010/30/EU).[228]

150. The scope of the Law of Georgia on Energy Efficiency includes a horizontal (cross-sectoral) policy that impacts public and private sectors and is related to energy services and their monitoring, measurement and confirmation,[229] as well as specific sectors: private building, including building for commercial purposes, and the sectors of industry, energy production, transformation, transmission and distribution.[230]

151. It also defines the obligations and responsibility measures of public and private institutions, household customers, energy service providers, and other industry and economic sectors in the process of energy consumption efficiency, energy saving, and the market development of energy services.[231]

152. The energy efficiency policy provides the creation of a legislative framework for energy efficiency, determines national targets for energy efficiency and energy saving and eliminates barriers that hinder the efficiency of energy supply and consumption and the achievement of the national energy-saving target set by the National Energy Efficiency Action Plan (NEEAP).

153. Functionally, the law aims to: (a) increase energy savings, energy supply security and energy independence, as well as to maximally eliminate barriers to improving energy efficiency in the energy market; (b) determine the general legal basis for the measures required to promote and implement energy efficiency in the

228. Article 300, Annex XXV, EU-Georgia Association Agreement, Art. 2, Energy Community Accession Protocol.
229. Article 2(1)(a), No. 5898-SS Law of Georgia on Energy Efficiency, 21 May 2020.
230. Article 2(1)(b), *ibid.*
231. Article 2(2), *ibid.*

country in order to ensure the achievement of the goals set out in the Protocol on the Accession of Georgia to the EnCT; (c) establish a procedure for developing a national energy efficiency target; (d) establish a procedure for adopting an energy efficiency action plan; (e) establish an energy efficiency commitment scheme and/or alternative policy measures to ensure energy savings; (f) implement an energy efficiency policy, its coordination, control, supervision and monitoring in the country.[232]

§1. Energy Efficiency Institutional Framework

154. First, the MoESD is responsible for developing the relevant legal framework and facilitating its implementation,[233] as well as implementing energy efficiency policies through the development and implementation of key directives, strategies, action plans and state programmes, within the scope of its competence, in coordination with public and state agencies and the private sector.[234]

155. The scope of responsibility of the Ministry also extends to developing the NEEAP, which shall determine the national energy-saving target, and submit it to the GoG for approval.[235] The MoESD determines appropriate measures to improve energy efficiency and promote its implementation.[236] The Ministry further encourages investment facilitation within the scope of its competence in order to improve energy efficiency[237] and represent Georgia in relevant international organizations.[238]

156. The functions of the Ministry are so extensive that it guarantees the implementation, enforcement, supervision and control of energy efficiency standards. In addition, beyond promotion and implementation of activities, it can be said that the role of the Ministry is highlighted in the development of one of the most important, the NEEAP, which is submitted to the Government on a three-year basis.[239] To define the functions of the Ministry in more detail, we need to follow the record of the law.

157. The Ministry also ensures: (a) the introduction of an energy management system and an energy audit; (b) the quality control of energy efficient devices and energy services; (c) the establishment of energy performance certification rules for energy auditors and persons who implement energy management, and the development and deployment of an energy performance certificate issuer, and technical

232. Article 1, *ibid.*
233. Article 4(b), *ibid.*
234. Article 4(a), *ibid.*
235. Article 4(c), *ibid.*
236. Article 4(d), *ibid.*
237. Article 4(e), *ibid.*
238. Article 4(f), *ibid.*
239. Article 4(6), *ibid.*

inspector certification programmes; (d) the development of a methodology for calculating energy savings achieved through measures taken at the national level, and a methodology for calculating energy savings achieved through individual measures; (e) the confirmation of an energy-saving target achieved by an energy consumer by providing energy services; (f) the development and approval of the procedures for reporting on the implementation of energy efficiency improvement measures and on achieved energy savings; (g) creating, updating and monitoring of a relevant register; (h) the implementation of a detailed assessment of the potential for the application of high-efficiency cogeneration, and efficient central heating and cooling, and the implementation of cost-effectiveness analysis; (i) the implementation and encouragement/facilitation of pilot (demonstration) projects; (j) the introduction of training programmes and energy consultation programmes and raising awareness activities; (k) the facilitation of the functioning of the energy services market.[240]

158. Starting with the implementation of the NEEAP,[241] the MoESD controls and supervises energy savings achieved within an energy efficiency commitment scheme and/or through alternative policy measures[242] as well as the activities of energy auditors and experts included in the list of experts developed in accordance with the procedures established by the law.[243] Controlling and supervising duties likewise apply to the implementation of an energy audit by enterprises of the first category,[244] the status of the introduction of a certified energy management system and/or a formal and certified environmental management system.[245] Most importantly, the MoESD takes responsibility for the compliance of an energy audit report with the requirements of the legislation of Georgia.[246]

159. The MoESD also shall, in the case of the violation of the requirements of the relevant legislation, draw up a protocol for an administrative offence and make a decision on imposing an administrative sanction/penalty.[247] Further, in relation to the Energy Labeling Law, MoESD should establish the compliance of the energy labelling procedure of an energy consumption product with the requirements of the legislation of Georgia in accordance with the requirements of the Law of Georgia on Energy Labelling.[248]

160. The activities of the MoESD are not only outlined by the above-mentioned functions, but it is also responsible for checking an energy-saving target achieved by an energy consumer through providing energy services for the purpose of its

240. Article 6(2), *ibid.*
241. Article 6(3)(a.a), *ibid.*
242. Article 6(3)(a.b), *ibid.*
243. Article 6(3)(a.c), *ibid.*
244. Article 6(3)(a.d), *ibid.*
245. Article 6(3)(a.e), *ibid.*
246. Article 6(3)(a.f), *ibid.*
247. Article 6(3)(b), *ibid.*
248. Article 6(3)(c), *ibid.*

verification.[249] The Ministry systematically monitors energy savings[250] and analyses annually the energy consumption by administrative bodies.[251] It is noteworthy that MoESD develops guidelines and recommendations for energy saving and energy efficiency measures for administrative bodies, individual users, and/or consumer groups[252] and submits reports in accordance with the purposes of the Energy Efficiency Law.[253] Maximizing its functions, MoESD issues administrative acts for the purpose of exercising the rights defined and fulfilling the duties provided for by the Energy Efficiency Law.[254]

161. When it comes to implementing the energy efficiency policy, the GoG shall consider the public benefit in order to achieve the following goals: (a) to take measures to determine prices reflecting the real value of energy so that the motivation of end users to implement energy efficient measures is not reduced; (b) to approve the NEEAP submitted by the Ministry; (c) to play an exemplary role in the implementation of measures to improve energy efficiency; (d) to promote the implementation of measures to improve energy efficiency by end users by developing financial instruments; (e) to strengthen international and regional cooperation; (f) to run information campaigns.[255]

§2. Energy Efficiency Policy

162. As mentioned above, the country's energy efficiency policy creates the specific legislative framework for energy efficiency, determines national targets for energy efficiency and energy saving, and eliminates barriers that hinder the efficiency of energy supply and consumption and the achievement of the national energy-saving target set by the NEEAP.

163. Furthermore, the implementation of energy efficiency policies shall involve various measures and initiatives, including: (a) the identification of projects, and the determination of technical assistance and granting of distribution schemes; (b) the adoption of regulatory norms for the energy efficiency of buildings on the basis of the legislation of Georgia, including the approval of a procedure for the certification of the energy efficiency of buildings, and raising qualifications in the construction sector; (c) deepening the knowledge of the business community, establishing procedures for energy audits and energy management systems, and raising the qualifications of energy auditors and energy service providers; (d) raising the level of knowledge and the experience of end users in energy efficiency, including entrepreneurial entities and administrative bodies in the field of production and trade; (e) the establishment of energy efficient public procurement practices; (f) improving

249. Article 6(3)(d), *ibid.*
250. Article 6(3)(e), *ibid.*
251. Article 6(3)(f), *ibid.*
252. Article 6(3)(g), *ibid.*
253. Article 6(3)(h), *ibid.*
254. Article 6(3)(i), *ibid.*
255. Article 4(3), *ibid.*

energy efficiency in energy conversion in the transmission and distribution sectors, which involves reducing electric power and/or natural gas losses in networks, and increasing the efficiency of natural gas power plants, by switching to combined cycle power plants; (g) improving the energy efficiency of final energy consumption devices, including lighting, cars, pumps, engines and plant boilers; (h) the initiation of the introduction of mechanisms for the implementation of financial incentives and tax concessions in order to promote energy efficiency measures; (i) the introduction of qualification, accreditation and certification schemes in industry, construction, and other relevant sectors, for the purposes of supervision and reporting.[256]

256. Article 4(2), *ibid.*

Chapter 2. Scope of the Law of Georgia on Energy Efficiency of Buildings

164. The Law of Georgia on Energy Efficiency of Buildings is fundamentally different insofar as it is more of a specific nature. Compared to the general energy efficiency framework, the law reflects more distinct aims and objectives, namely, it aspires to promote the rational use of energy resources and to improve the energy efficiency of buildings by taking into account the external climate and local conditions of buildings, the demand for indoor climate conditions and cost-effectiveness.[257]

165. The procedure for certifying the energy performance of buildings shall be approved and the procedure for placing the energy performance certificate and the information to be included in it shall be determined by a normative act of the GoG.[258] Along with the assessment of the energy efficiency of a building and the values of minimum energy performance requirements,[259] the energy performance certificate also consists of recommendations on the cost-optimal improvement of the energy performance of a building or a part of a building, when such improvement is not rational towards the requirements established for energy performance.[260]

166. For the purposes of the law, definite criteria are specified for the type of buildings that are subject to mandatory certification, such as a new building or a part of a building;[261] an existing building that is for sale or rent/lease;[262] a part of an existing building which is for sale or rent/lease;[263] a building used by a public institution the total area of which is more than 500 m^2 and that is often visited by outsiders, and from 30 June 2026, for a building used by a public institution, the total area of which is more than 250 m^2 and that is often visited by outsiders.[264] The failure to implement the certification of the performance of a building or a part of a building shall result in the imposition of a fine on the owner of a building or a part of a building accordingly.[265]

---

257. Article 1(1), No. 5900-SS The Law of Georgia on Energy Efficiency of Buildings, 21 May 2020.
258. Article 7(1), *ibid.*
259. Article 7(2)(a), *ibid.*
260. Article 7(2)(b), *ibid.*
261. Article 7(3)(a), *ibid.*
262. Article 7(3)(b), *ibid.*
263. Article 7(3)(c), *ibid.*
264. Article 7(3)(d), *ibid.*
265. Article 12, *ibid.*

Part V. Regulatory Framework Concerning Renewable Energy

Chapter 1. Introduction

167. The regulatory framework concerning renewable energy in Georgia is mainly established by the sector-specific Law of Georgia on Promoting the Production and Use of Energy from Renewable Sources (hereinafter 'Renewable Energy Law'). At the declaratory as well as the functional level, the renewable energy policy in Georgia should be in conformity with the EU and its legislation and, therefore, the Law of Georgia on Promoting the Production and Use of Energy from Renewable Sources was adopted on 20 December 2019 in compliance with Directive 2009/28/EC of the European Parliament and of the Council of 23 April 2009 on the promotion of the use of energy from renewable sources.

§1. Scope of the Law of Georgia on Promoting the Production and Use of Energy from Renewable Sources

168. According to Article 1(1) of the Law of Georgia on Promoting the Production and Use of Energy from Renewable Sources, the purpose of the law is to establish a legal basis for the promotion, facilitation and use of energy from renewable sources[266] and to set mandatory national targets for the overall share of energy from renewable sources in gross final consumption of energy, as well as in transport.[267] The law acknowledges that the premise of using RES is becoming even more robust as exploitation of traditional resources has a detrimental effect on climate and environment. In order to duly accomplish the objectives set forth by the law, the GoG installs mandatory, overall national targets and measures for the use of energy from renewable sources.

169. In order for the Government to efficiently enforce renewable energy policy, it is essential to deploy various support schemes. In domestic legislation, a support scheme is defined as any instrument, scheme or mechanism applied by Georgia separately or with EnC CP/group of CPs, that promotes the use of energy from

266. Article 1.1(a), No. 5652 Law of Georgia on Promoting the Production and Use of Energy from Renewable Sources, 20 Dec. 2019.
267. Article 1.1(b), *ibid.*

renewable sources in Georgia by reducing the cost of that energy, increasing the price at which it can be sold, or increasing, by means of a renewable energy obligation or otherwise, the volume of such energy purchased.[268]

170. The support schemes may materialize in the form of investment aids, tax exemptions or reductions, tax refunds, renewable energy obligation support schemes including those using green certificates, and direct price support schemes including feed-in tariffs and premium payments.

171. Besides the above-mentioned support schemes, in order to facilitate the use of energy from renewable sources, the GoG and the competent authorities of one or more EnC CPs may cooperate on all types of joint projects relating to the production of electricity, heating or cooling from RES. The cooperation may as well involve private operators.[269]

172. It is noteworthy that according to Article 6(1), Georgia and EnC CPs may agree on and may make arrangements for the statistical transfer of a specified amount of energy from renewable sources from Georgia to EnC CP or vice versa.[270] A statistical transfer shall not affect the achievement of the national target of Georgia, and it may have a duration of one or more years.[271]

173. The measures taken shall be notified to the EnC Secretariat.[272] Moreover, Article 9(1) of the respective law relates to joint projects between Georgia and third countries. As stipulated, 'Georgia separately or with Energy Community Contracting Party/Parties may cooperate with one or more third countries on all types of joint projects regarding the production of electricity from renewable energy sources'.[273] This type of cooperation may also involve private operators.

174. It has to be emphasized that in relation to third countries, Georgia is able to only cooperate on joint projects that relate to the production of electricity, while with regards to EnC CPs, the collaboration also covers heating and cooling issues. In case Georgia is willing to cooperate with one or more EnC CPs, the GoG shall notify the EnC Secretariat about the joint programme.

175. In compliance with Directive 2009/28/EC, the GoG shall ensure that the share of energy from renewable sources, calculated in accordance with this law, in gross final consumption of energy in 2030 is at least its overall national target for the share of energy from renewable sources in that year, as set out in the third column of the table in point one of Annex I (Law of Georgia on Promoting the Use of

268. Article 2.2(k), *ibid.*
269. Article 7(1), *ibid.*
270. Article 6(1), *ibid.*
271. Article 6, *ibid.*
272. Article 6(4), *ibid.*
273. Article 9(1), *ibid.*

Energy from Renewable Sources).[274] Promoting and encouraging energy efficiency and energy-saving measures are essential, so as to achieve the above-mentioned objectives.

176. Furthermore, the GoG in accordance with respective laws shall apply support schemes and/or cooperate with different EnC CPs, as well as with third countries in order to achieve their overall national targets.[275] In order to achieve overall national targets, Article 4 of Directive 2009/28/EC sets the obligation on states to adopt national renewable energy action plans.[276]

177. Consequently, in accordance with Directive 2009/28/EC, Article 4(1) of the Law of Georgia on Promoting the Production and Use of Energy from Renewable Sources requires the GoG to approve by its decree a ten-year national renewable energy action plan, which is elaborated by the MoESD.[277]

§2. Georgian National Energy and Water Supply Regulatory Commission

178. The GNERC shall ensure that any rules concerning the authorization, certification and licensing procedures that are applied to plants and associated transmission and distribution network infrastructures for the production of electricity, heating or cooling from RES, and to the process of transformation of biomass into biofuels or other energy products are proportionate and necessary.[278] The GoG shall ensure that information on support measures is made available to all relevant actors, in particular to consumers, builders, installers, architects, and suppliers of heating, cooling and electricity equipment and systems and of vehicles compatible with the use of energy from renewable sources.[279]

179. In order to prove to final customers the share or quantity of energy from renewable sources in an energy supplier's energy mix, GNERC shall ensure that the proof of origin of electricity produced from RES can be guaranteed as such within the meaning of this law, in accordance with objective, transparent and non-discriminatory criteria. To this end, the GNERC shall, by its decree, approve the rules for issuing guarantees of origin for electricity, heating and cooling produced from RES.[280]

---

274. Article 3(1), *ibid.*
275. Article 3(4), *ibid.*
276. *See* I. Samkharadze, *Europeanization of Energy Law and Policy Beyond the Member States: The Case of Georgia*, 130 Elsevier Energy Pol'y J. 189 (2019).
277. Article 4(1), No. 5652 Law of Georgia on Promoting the Production and Use of Energy from Renewable Sources, 20 Dec. 2019.
278. Article 13(1), *ibid.*
279. Article 14(1), *ibid.*
280. Article 15(1), *ibid.*

180. In order to supervise and assess the performance of respective obligations, Article 21(1) of the Renewable Energy Law keeps accountable the GoG to submit a report to the Secretariat on progress in the promotion and use of energy from renewable sources by 31 December 2024 and every two years thereafter.[281]

281. Article 21(1), *ibid.*

Chapter 2. Cooperation Mechanisms

§1. SUPPORT SCHEMES

181. By setting a national target for the share of energy from RES in total final energy consumption, Georgia has committed itself to achieving this goal through appropriate mechanisms.

182. In turn, the Renewable Energy Law defines Support Scheme as any instrument, scheme or mechanism applied by Georgia separately or with EnC CP/group of CPs, that promotes the use of energy from renewable sources in Georgia by reducing the cost of that energy, increasing the price at which it can be sold, or increasing, by means of a renewable energy obligation or otherwise, the volume of such energy purchased. This includes, but is not restricted to, investment aid, tax exemptions or reductions, tax refunds, renewable energy obligation support schemes including those using green certificates, and direct price support schemes including feed-in tariffs and premium payments.[282]

183. According to the law, the GoG may apply the following measures: (a) support schemes; (b) measures of cooperation between different EnC CPs and/or with third countries for achieving their overall national targets.[283] As a matter of course, the MoESD develops and submits to the GoG for adoption of the support schemes.[284] The Government itself defines the technical specifications which must be met by renewable energy equipment and systems in order to benefit from support schemes.[285] The Government shall also submit a report to the Secretariat on progress in the promotion and use of energy from renewable sources by 31 December 2024 and every two years thereafter.[286] The support schemes must be approved by the GoG within twelve months of the adoption of the law.[287]

184. Determining the national and international character of the support scheme, Georgia and one or more EnC CPs may decide, on a voluntary basis, to join or partly coordinate their national support schemes.[288]

185. The new framework energy law, described closely in previous chapters, also draws a parallel and creates a framework for the promotion of renewable energy, which together with 'The Law of Georgia on Promoting the Production and Use of Energy from Renewable Sources' promotes the production of energy through renewable energy methods.

282. Article 2(1)(n), *ibid.*
283. Article 3(4), *ibid.*
284. Article 11(1), *ibid.*
285. Article 13(3), *ibid.*
286. Article 20(1), *ibid.*
287. Article 21(5)(c), *ibid.*
288. Article 11(2), *ibid.*

186. The Concept of the Georgian Electricity Market also promotes implementation of support schemes under the Law of Georgia on Encouragement of Production and Use of Energy from Renewable Sources.[289] The market concept defines the concept of wholesale public services and their specific commitments in the field of renewable energy, such as financial settlement within the relevant support scheme with producers participating in the renewable energy and other support schemes and promoting integration into the organized market.[290]

187. Defined by the law, producers using renewable energy and producers using other support schemes themselves (or through a person provided by the contract) ensure the sale of electricity generated by them in the organized market. The fee provided by the support scheme for them will be reimbursed by the wholesale public service organization.[291] The procedure for forming the required fund shall be established by a resolution of the GoG on the organization of wholesale public services.

§2. Statistical Transfers

188. The main legislative framework for the use and promotion of renewable resources defines Statistical Transfer as a transfer of a certain amount of energy from renewable sources through a green certificate by Georgia to one or more CPs of the EnC or by one or more CPs of the Energy Union to Georgia (purchase included). As a result, the transmitted energy is added to the mandatory overall national target values of the receiving party and subtracted from the mandatory national total target values of the transmitting party.[292]

189. Georgia and EnC CPs may agree on and may make arrangements for the statistical transfer of a specified amount of energy from renewable sources from Georgia to EnC CP or vice versa.[293] The transferred quantity shall be deducted from the amount of energy from renewable sources and added to the amount of energy from renewable sources that are taken into account in measuring compliance by the country making or accepting the transfer respectively, with the requirements of mandatory overall national target.[294] A statistical transfer shall not affect the achievement of the national target of Georgia when making the transfer.[295] Statistical transfer may have a duration of one or more years.[296]

289. Article 1(1)(e), No. 246 Resolution of the Government of Georgia, 'The Concept for the Georgian Electricity Market'.
290. Article 10, *ibid.*
291. Article 11(4), *ibid.*
292. Article 1(1)(x), No. 5652 Law of Georgia on Promoting the Production and Use of Energy from Renewable Sources, 20 Dec. 2019.
293. Article 6(1), *ibid.*
294. Article 6(1)(a)(b), *ibid.*
295. Article 6(2), *ibid.*
296. Article 6(3), *ibid.*

190. These measures shall be notified to the EnC Secretariat no later than three months after the end of each year in which they have an effect. The information sent to the EnC Secretariat shall include information regarding the quantity and price of the energy involved.[297] Statistical transfers shall become effective only after all EnC CPs involved in the transfer have notified about the statistical transfer to the EnC Secretariat.[298]

191. It is important to note that the same rules apply to the statistical transfers with the EU Member State from the territory of the EU Member State to Georgia or from Georgia to the EU Member State.[299]

297. *Ibid.*
298. Article 6(4), No. 5652 Law of Georgia on Promoting the Production and Use of Energy from Renewable Sources, 20 Dec. 2019.
299. Article 6(5), *ibid.*

Part VI. Interaction Between Energy Law and Environmental Law

Chapter 1. Introduction

192. The interaction between energy law and environmental law can be assessed by the impact of commercial activities on the overall environment performed by the energy sector. Fundamentally, energy law is economic in its nature aspiring to upsurge resources' commercial benefits for a certain commercial interest, whereas environmental law tends more to avoid harmful impacts on the environment by imposing a number of restrictions and obliging any entity that may have a negative impact on the environment.

193. Energy generation is directed towards the utilization and transformation of natural resources, and therefore all energy generation activities have environmental consequences. That is why the interdependence of these two fields has been established as they actively seek a productive coexistence. However, environmental law, by its very nature, is way more internationalized than energy law. Energy law is bound by the framework of environmental regulations, which provides strict adherence to the principles of national and international sustainable development. In fact, Georgia has ratified all important agreements in the field of environmental protection; therefore, the common framework of these agreements ensures the development of a sustainable development policy.

194. For the purposes of environmental law, public health safeguards as well as protecting the ecosystem from any harm, caused by energy activities, turned out to be much harder to perform than expected. Energy law must mitigate the impact on the environment and take more responsibility for the after-effects, as economic interest alone cannot cope with a condition caused by a shortage of non-renewable resources, air pollution, climate change, etc. Energy generation has an enormous impact on the environment; in consequence, it is for this reason that these two fields aspire to establish close linkages.

195. Adverse effects of the low efficiency of traditional energy regeneration on the environment[300] occur throughout their processing cycle, which is directly related to emissions, soil damage, water pollution, climate change, GHGs emitted into the

300. Coal, oil and natural gas.

atmosphere by burning fossil fuels or any other type of harm caused by energy generation. The current consumption of non-renewable energy resources is unsustainable, and it needs to be replaced by renewable energy[301] resources, hence energy law's regulatory space is crucial in the energy transition processes, and this is the exact point where the functional dependence and collaborative nature of environmental law come into force and play a crucial role in tackling modern energy threats and challenges.

301. Hydro, Solar, Wind, Biomass, Atomic (or nuclear) and Geothermal Energy.

Chapter 2. Institutional Framework

196. Integrating environmental issues into other sectoral policies requires Georgian ministries and the Government as a whole to establish and refine the local legislative framework in this regard and to comply with internationally recognized legal obligations.

197. In Georgia, the core segment of environmental policy and legislation has been developed by the MoEPA. It plays an immeasurably large role in environmental activities and also, from an administrative point of view, is part of the development and implementation of key policies. MoEPA issues permits and, above all, partially coordinates the implementation of international agreements regarding environmental law.

198. Government, the Parliament of Georgia, MoESD, and MoEPA are key actors concerning energy sector development and environmental protection. Additionally, the Ministry of Regional Development and Infrastructure of Georgia, Ministry of Labor, Health and Social Defence of Georgia, Ministry of Finance of Georgia, Ministry of Internal Affairs and self-governing units share competences in the energy sector and environmental protection.

Chapter 3. Legal Framework of Environmental Law of Relevance to the Energy Sector

199. The primary source that forms the environmental legislative framework is the 1996 Law of Georgia on Environmental Protection (hereinafter 'the law'),[302] which has been revised plenty of times. To date, it, along with other new laws, equally reflects the influence of EU law. It should be emphasized that the law aspires to define the principles and norms of legal relations in the field of environmental protection[303] with the equally essential rationale to protect the basic human rights established by the Constitution of Georgia in the field of environmental protection – to live in an environment harmless to health and to enjoy the natural and cultural environment.[304]

200. Considering the basic principles of protection and rational use of the environment by the state,[305] the law ensures to promote the conservation of biodiversity, rare, endemic, endangered species of flora and fauna characteristic of the country, the protection of the marine environment and the maintenance of ecological balance.[306] Along with preserving and protecting unique landscapes and ecosystems,[307] environmental law framework sets the goal to legally ensure the solution of common global and regional problems in the field of environmental protection[308] and desires to provide the conditions for sustainable development of the country.[309]

201. Moreover, in the light of clear, concise and unconditional regulation, the law stipulates that protecting and maintaining a safe environment for human health[310] should be defined as the main task of the environmental framework. Further, legally ensuring protection from harmful environmental impacts;[311] maintaining and improving the quality of the environment;[312] integrating the ecological, economic and social interests of the society (harmonious harmony);[313] managing the use of natural resources, taking into account the potential of the environment and the principles of sustainable development[314] and efficient functioning of a unified system of regulation of genetically modified living organisms[315] shall be equally considered the constituent pillars.

302. No. 519-1 Law of Georgia on Environmental Protection, 10 Dec. 1996.
303. Article 3(1)(a), *ibid.*
304. Article 3(1)(b), *ibid.*
305. Article 3(1)(c), *ibid.*
306. Article 3(1)(d), *ibid.*
307. Article 3(1)(e), *ibid.*
308. Article 3(1)(f), *ibid.*
309. Article 3(1)(g), *ibid.*
310. Article 3(2)(a), *ibid.*
311. Article 3(2)(b), *ibid.*
312. Article 3(2)(c), *ibid.*
313. Article 3(2)(d), *ibid.*
314. Article 3(2)(e), *ibid.*
315. Article 3(2)(f), *ibid.*

202. Ratification of the AA, explained in detail above, created a long-term perspective for national energy and environment policy development. Chapter VI of the AA regulates the Energy and Environmental Sector Cooperation. The agreement hereby states that the cooperation should be based on the principles of partnership, mutual interest, transparency and predictability and shall aim at market integration and regulatory convergence in the energy sector, taking into account the need to ensure access to secure, environmentally friendly and affordable energy.[316]

203. Regarding environmental cooperation, the agreement determines that the cooperation shall aim at preserving, protecting, improving and rehabilitating the quality of the environment, protecting human health, sustainable utilization of natural resources and promoting measures at international level to deal with regional or global environmental problems, including in the areas of: (a) environmental governance and horizontal issues, including strategic planning, EIA and Strategic Environmental Assessment (SEA), education and training, monitoring and environmental information systems, inspection and enforcement, environmental liability, combating environmental crime, transboundary cooperation, public access to environmental information, decision-making processes and effective administrative and judicial review procedures; (b) air quality; (c) water quality and resource management, including flood risk management, water scarcity and droughts as well as marine environment; (d) waste management; (e) nature protection, including forestry and conservation of biological diversity; (f) industrial pollution and industrial hazards; and (g) chemicals management.[317] Cooperation also aims at integrating environmental principles into policy areas other than environmental policy.[318]

204. Pursuant to the AA, Georgia has come a long way in making changes in both energy and environmental sectors, and gradually, a national legislative model closer to European legislation is being created.[319] Interaction between energy and environmental laws is clearly reflected in the newly adopted laws, decrees and respective strategies.

205. According to the 'Government Program for 2019–2020 Performance report',[320] during the time period of 2019–2020 in the energy sector, Georgia has adopted: Law of Georgia on Energy and Water Supply; Law of Georgia on Energy Labeling; Law of Georgia on Promoting the Production and Use of Energy from Renewable Sources; Law of Georgia on Energy Efficiency; Law of Georgia on Energy Efficiency of Buildings; Resolution on 'Electricity Market Model Concept'.

316. Article 297, EU-Georgia Association Agreement.
317. Article 302(1), *ibid.*
318. Article 302(2), *ibid.*
319. Article 300, *ibid.*
320. Government Program for 2019–2020 Performance report (in Georgian): http://gov.ge/files/424_76377_223408_1.3%E1%83%A1%E1%83%90%E1%83%9B%E1%83%97%E1%83%90%E1%83%95%E1%83%A0%E1%83%9D%E1%83%91%E1%83%9D%E1%83%9E%E1%83%A0%E1%83%9D%E1%83%92%E1%83%A0%E1%83%90%E1%83%9B%E1%83%98%E1%83%A1%E1%83%90%E1%83%9C%E1%83%92%E1%83%90%E1%83%A0%E1%83%98%E1%83%A8%E1%83%98.pdf, accessed on 11 Sep. 2020.

206. In parallel to these processes, the following developments took place in the environmental sector:

- A CCC has been set up.
- The Forest Code has been adopted in the field of sustainable forest management.
- Law on Environmental Liability has been developed.
- An amendment to the Law of Georgia on Atmospheric Air Protection was prepared and approved by the Parliament of Georgia.
- During the reporting period, a draft law on water resources management was developed, which is in line with the EU Water Framework Directive.
- A law on biodiversity is being developed.

207. Apart from this, technical regulations have been adopted on: 'Batteries and Automotive Battery Waste Management', 'Waste Management of Electrical and Electronic Equipment', 'Waste Oil Management', 'Tire Waste Management', while the regulations on 'Packaging Waste Management' and 'the Management of Decommissioned Vehicles' are under consideration to pass.[321]

321. For detailed review, please visit the registry of the Parliament of Georgia: http://www.parliament.ge/ge/kanonmdebloba, accessed on 22 Sep. 2020.

Chapter 4. The Review of Different Legal Instruments

§1. RES LAW

208. The Law of Georgia on Promoting the Production and Use of Energy from Renewable Sources substantially reinterprets the idea of sustainable development[322] in the field of Georgian energy law. The percentage of renewable energy target consumption has never been set by domestic law before. It establishes a legal basis for the promotion, facilitation and use of energy from renewable sources[323] and sets a mandatory national target for the overall share of energy from renewable sources in gross final consumption of energy, as well as in transport.[324]

209. The Government by its decree approves a ten-year national renewable energy action plan, elaborated by the MoESD. The Ministry is bound to renew the action plan every two years and submit it for approval to the GoG.[325] It should be noted that the national total target indicator of the share of energy from renewable sources in total final energy consumption, by 2030, is set at 35%.[326]

§2. ENVIRONMENTAL ASSESSMENT CODE

210. In essence, the Environmental Assessment Code may not be distinct from other environmental laws insofar as it also aims to protect the environment and human health. Nevertheless, the key drivers for the adoption of Environmental Assessment Code in Georgia on 7 June 2017 are to introduce innovations in the field of environment, namely, the procedures for EIA, SEA, transboundary EIA, and public participation in decision-making, as well as the conduct of expert examinations.[327]

211. The main purposes of the Code include regulating the relations in the cases where EIAs are required and protecting the environment and public health. It consists of eight chapters: General Provisions (I); Environmental Decision (II); Strategic EIA (III); Public Participation in Environmental Decision-Making Contemplated under the Code (IV); Assessment of Transboundary Environmental Impact (V); Expert Commission (VI); Supervision and Responsibilities in the Field of EIAs (VII); and Transitional and Final Provisions (VIII).

212. The Code additionally clarifies the interaction between energy law and environmental law; in other words, the law sets the norm for SEA. According to the law, the purpose of a SEA is to: (a) minimize adverse effects on the environment

322. Article 29, Constitution of Georgia, 24 Aug. 1995.
323. Article 1(1)(a), No. 5652 Law of Georgia on Promoting the Production and Use of Energy from Renewable Sources, 20 Dec. 2019.
324. Article 1(1)(b), *ibid.*
325. Article 4(1), *ibid.*
326. Annex I, 1, *ibid.*
327. Article 1(2), N890-IIS Environmental Assessment Code, 1 Jun. 2017.

and human health; (b) ensure public participation in the preparation and adoption/approval of a strategic document; (c) take account of environmental and human health aspects in the decision-making related to a strategic document; (d) perform a transboundary EIA procedure in the process of the decision-making related to a strategic document, where relevant.[328]

213. The performance of the SEA shall be mandatory in the case of a strategic document and a major change to a strategic document which establishes a framework for future development, namely in energy, transport, waste management, and industry sectors.[329]

§3. Law of Georgia on Ambient Air Protection

214. Another important legislative worth considering is the Law of Georgia on Atmospheric Air Protection,[330] which will be rigorously scrutinized in Part VII below. The law has been revised several times, in order to comply with EU Legislation,[331] and the current version responds to the modern challenges that are equally represented in the field of energy and environment at the international level.

215. The law ensures the protection of ambient air, as one of the main components of the environment, in accordance with environmental and economic interests of society and takes into account the interests of present and future generations. It also provides a legal framework to resolve common global and regional problems in the field of ambient air protection. Therefore, the law stipulates the following: 'The regulation of ambient air pollution with harmful substances includes classification of and accounting for pollution types and pollution sources, restriction of emissions of harmful substances from stationary sources of pollution into the ambient air and other requirements prescribed by this law, which are intended to attain, maintain and improve an ambient air condition that is safe for human health and the natural environment'.[332]

§4. Waste Management Code and the Law of Georgia on Import, Export and Transit of Waste

216. The role of the interaction between energy and environmental law can also be clearly seen in the Waste Management Code[333] and the Law of Georgia on

328. Article 19, *ibid.*
329. Article 20(4), *ibid.*
330. No. 2116 Law of Georgia on Ambient Air Protection, 22 Jun. 1999.
331. 2008/50/EC Directive on the Ambient Air Quality and Cleaner Air for Europe of 21 May 2008 of the Council of the European Union; 2004/107/EC Directive on Arsenic, Cadmium, Mercury, Nickel and Polycyclic Aromatic Hydrocarbons in Ambient Air of 15 Dec. 2004.
332. Article 22, No. 2116 Law of Georgia on Ambient Air Protection, 22 Jun. 1999.
333. No. 2994-RS Waste Management Code, 26 Dec. 2014.

Import, Export and Transit of Waste.[334] The Code aims to prevent or reduce waste, its adverse impact[335] and establishes effective mechanisms for waste management.[336] Mainly, the law aspires to reduce damage caused by the consumption of resources and aims to make use of the resources in a more efficient way.[337] Furthermore, the code realizes its 'Punitive Function' by invoking a 'Polluter Pays'[338] principle.

217. The Law of Georgia on Import, Export and Transit of Waste is a *lex specialis* and establishes general rules on the import, export and transit of waste, as well as the rules for issuing the relevant licence by MoESD,[339] as waste is considered a special category of material, whether it is hazardous or not.[340]

§5. Forest Code of Georgia

218. According to the Ministry of Environment Protection and Agriculture, the forest area of Georgia is 3,124.2 hectares and is currently fully state-owned. Legal Entity of Public Law (LEPL), the National Forest Agency, manages 1,996.9 hectares of forest, while the 596.2 hectares of forest is managed by the LEPL Agency of Protected Areas. The average amount of timber per hectare of Georgian forests (forest density factor) is about 107 m^3, and the total annual timber growth is about 3.6 million m^3. Lack of roads in forests makes it impossible to extract raw materials from the depths, which makes it technically difficult to extract timber. It is estimated that for energy purposes, no more than 15%–20% of the annual growth of complete forest timber can be used. According to the results obtained based on these and other assumptions, the energy potential of all forests in Georgia is about 550,000 m^3 leading to the wood biomass being one of the main energy resources of Georgia.[341]

219. The newly adopted Forest Code of Georgia[342] deeply embedded in the universal sustainable development processes under the 2030 Agenda[343] aims to ensure targeted and rational use of forest resources and other natural potential of forest.[344] The Code regulates legal relations associated with tending, protection, restoration

334. No. 631 The Law of Georgia on Import, Export and Transit of Waste, 8 Feb. 1995.
335. Article 1(2)(a), No. 2994-RS Waste Management Code, 26 Dec. 2014.
336. Article 1(2)(b), *ibid.*
337. Article 1(2)(c), *ibid.*
338. Article 5(2)(b), *ibid.*
339. Article 4^1, No. 631 The Law of Georgia on Import, Export and Transit of Waste, 8 Feb. 1995. Article 29, No. 1775 Law of Georgia on Licenses and Permits, 24 Jun. 2005.
340. Article 3(1), No. 631 The Law of Georgia on Import, Export and Transit of Waste, 8 Feb. 1995.
341. The Energy Strategy of Georgia 2020–2030.
342. No. 5949-SS Forest Code of Georgia, 22 May 2020.
343. Agenda 2030 for sustainable Development: https://sdgs.un.org/2030agenda, accessed on 07 Aug. 2023.
344. Article 1, 2(c), No. 5949-SS Forest Code of Georgia, 22 May 2020.

and use of the forest fund of Georgia and its resources. Its goals include: (a) protecting fundamental human rights and law enforcement in the field of forest relations; (b) conducting tending, protection and restoration of forests in order to maintain and improve climatic, water regulating, protective, cultural, recreational and other natural useful properties; (c) conducting tending and protection for future generations and regulating harmonized interrelations between unique natural and cultural environment and its specific components thereof including vegetation and wildlife, biodiversity, landscape, cultural and natural monuments located in forest, and the rare endangered plant species of plants, etc.; (d) establishing the rights and obligations of forest users in the field of forest relations; (e) meeting environmental, economic, social and cultural needs of Georgia and its population through targeted, comprehensive and rational utilization of the forest resources, on the basis of their scientifically substantiated potential; and (f) establishing the main principles of forest management. The code is divided into eight parts and one hundred and twenty articles.

Part VII. Law on Climate Change

Chapter 1. Introduction

220. Climate change, as a fast-emerging discipline, is developing at an astonishing pace in legal scholarship. This is due to its challenging nature as one of the biggest global threats to be responded to adequately worldwide, including Georgia. The country distinguished by its biodiversity and rich freshwater resources encounters serious risks of climate change adverse impact.[345] Climate mitigation and adaptation, therefore, become key priorities of the GoG putting special emphasis on integrating climate hazards into the country's core strategic planning.[346] In order to improve climate preparedness, Georgia is now endeavouring on adjusting national laws and policies aiming at increasing climate resilience and adaptative capacities as well as reducing GHG emissions and vulnerability of highly exposed communities.

221. It has on several occasions been acknowledged that Georgia envisages modernizing its obsolete or rather inconsistent national climate legislation in close cooperation with the EU. This process was accelerated in the aftermath of approving the landmark UNFCCC PA[347] committing Georgia to develop more ambitious climate targets complemented by fairness principles and robust monitoring and reporting. Although the Agreement has not been formally ratified by the Georgian Parliament, it still stands out as the legally binding instrument approved by the GoG on 21 February 2017. According to Article 7(1) of the Law of Georgia on International treaties, Georgia may express consent to be bound by treaties through: (a) signing the treaties; (b) exchanging the documents (notes) as parts of the treaty; (c) ratifying the treaties; (d) approving the treaties; (e) acceding to the treaties; (f) mutually agreeing to other means of consent to the treaties.[348] The implementation of the PA and the review of international climate commitment will largely be

345. Ministry of Environment and Natural Resources of Georgia, 2015. Third National Communication of Georgia to the UN Framework Convention on Climate Change (UNFCCC), Tbilisi, 13.
346. No. 2328 Ordinance of the Government of Georgia on approval of the National Strategy of the Sustainable Development Goals, 12 Nov. 2019.
347. UNFCCC, 'What Is the Paris Agreement?' https://unfccc.int/process-and-meetings/the-paris-agreement/what-is-the-paris-agreement, accessed on 9 Apr. 2020.
348. Article 7(1), No. 934 Law of Georgia on International Treaties of Georgia, 16 Oct. 1997.

dependent on the alignment of already-assumed obligations in national legislation and the legal harmonization of the EU climate action.[349]

222. The approximation of the EU climate action poses substantial challenges to Georgia's domestic climate legislation. It is not, however, pursued in a silo mode, but supported by the EU itself as an 'exporter' of climate rules and regulations. The EU does not only impose the set of legal obligations on Georgia, but it eases the heavy legal burden via the mechanics of bilateral and multilateral agreements – Association Agreement and EnCT – explained in the general introduction of the monograph. In other words, it is also called the Europeanization of Georgia's climate legal framework, when a top-down process translates change from the European level to the national one and stimulates the local agenda.

223. It is crucial to mention that Georgia is currently taking significant strides towards combatting climate change and ensuring a sustainable future by preparing a comprehensive climate law that aligns with the best international and European standards. This crucial undertaking holds immense importance for several compelling reasons. This potential legislative initiative showcases Georgia's dedication to global climate action, strengthens its integration into the EU, ensures its own resilience and development, and attracts vital investments. By embracing this crucial endeavour, Georgia paves the way for a sustainable future and contributes to the global fight against climate change.

224. As a country vulnerable to the impacts of climate change, including rising temperatures, changing precipitation patterns, and increased frequency of extreme weather events, Georgia needs effective legislation to build resilience, protect its citizens, and safeguard its natural resources. A comprehensive climate law would provide a strong foundation for the country to implement adaptation and mitigation measures, promote RES, and foster sustainable practices across sectors.

225. At the time of writing, the consultation document titled 'A Climate Law for Georgia a Green Paper to Explore Ideas' has been launched in early 2023 to start establishing a new process for creating legislation. The Georgian Parliament's Environmental Protection and Natural Resources Committee in close cooperation with the government is leading the process to define and create a draft Climate Law for Parliament to consider. The aim of the document is to consult with the Georgian community as widely as possible. Based on the involvement of public, the White Paper to create a draft Climate Law will be prepared in the course of 2023. Eventually, the draft Climate Law will be prepared to be the subject of rigorous and comprehensive impact assessments, including gender-specific needs and socio-economic aspects.[350]

349. *See* I. Samkharadze, *Changing Architecture of Georgian Renewable Energy Normative System: The Dos and Don'ts from the European Union*, 30(3) Eur. Energy & Envtl. L. Rev. 94–103 (2021).

350. For more information, *see*: https://www.wfd.org/press-releases/georgia-launches-work-climate-change-law, accessed on 27 Jun. 2023.

Chapter 2. Climate Stocktaking in Georgia

226. Despite Georgia's low level of GHG emissions per capita, the country considers itself a responsible member of the international community committed to combating climate change. That is why Georgia, as a non-Annex I party to UNFCCC, submitted its first international legally binding climate commitment – Intended Nationally Determined Contribution (INDC) to curb carbon emissions ahead of the breakthrough PA. In its INDC, Georgia has pledged to reduce GHG emissions unconditionally by 15% (with an additional 10% of conditionality) compared to the business-as-usual scenario by 2030.[351] It is of the highest significance to mention that in April 2021, the Georgian Government approved the updated targets of Nationally Determined Contribution as well as the Climate Strategy 2030 and the Strategy Action Plan 2021–2031.[352] According to the new trend, Georgia is committed to an unconditional limiting target of 35% below 1990 levels of its domestic total GHG emissions by 2030, which significantly boosts the hydrogen development perspectives in the country. Georgia is additionally committing to a target of 50%–57% of its total GHG emissions in case of international support. Prior to that, Georgia acceded to the UNFCCC in 1994 with its subsequent KP on 28 May 1999.[353]

227. Nevertheless, translating political pledges into national legal action is a challenge for Georgia. The country is not advanced in a climate-specific legal framework, and it does not operate comprehensive, dedicated legislation on climate change. There is no single climate legal act in place, and several sectoral laws and regulatory measures dealing with climate-related matters are scattered in the primary and secondary legislation. Given this, the harmonization of the domestic climate legislative framework and nationalization of the international commitments are of high relevance.

228. The aforenamed AA and EnCT are launching key legal pathways that are shaping climate change commitments at the local level. Pursuant to these instruments, Georgia is in a unique situation accepting the EU's climate *acquis* that transcends the national borders and is encapsulated in the Georgian regime. Accordingly, the country largely benefits from harmonizing the obsolete or rather uneven climate legislation. The specifics of the legal harmonization and the concrete impact of EU key climate legislation on Georgia are explored further in the next chapter.

---

351. *See* Georgia's INDC submitted on 25 Sep. 2015: https://www4.unfccc.int/sites/ndcstaging/PublishedDocuments/Georgia%20First/INDC_of_Georgia.pdf, accessed on 13 Apr. 2020.
352. Seven sectors and pledges on RE Advancement (hydro, solar, wind HPP technical and procedural support, Wind farm support).
353. The decree of the Parliament of Georgia on UNFCCC Kyoto Protocol, 28 May 1999.

Chapter 3. EU Climate Acquis and Their Influence on Georgian Legislation

§1. The Legal Nature

229. Upon entering into force on 1 July 2016, the bilateral Association Agreement became automatically a legal act incorporated into the Georgian legal system,[354] which has been explained in the general introduction. Therefore, the AA provisions covering two EU Regulations (Regulation (EC) No. 842/2006 on certain fluorinated GHGs and Regulation (EC) No. 1005/2009 on substances that deplete the ozone layer in the field of climate has got a strong legally binding status on Georgia.

230. Additionally, AA stresses the necessity of cooperation on climate change issues in the following spheres: mitigation and adaptation to climate change, carbon trade, integration into industrial policy on climate change issues and development of clean technologies.[355] While Article 310 of the AA refers to the Low Emissions Development Strategy, Nationally Appropriate Mitigation Actions and National Adaptation Programme of Action, Article 312 mandates the country 'to carry out approximation of its legislation to the EU acts and international instruments referred to in Annex XXVII'. The commitment to tackle climate change is also underscored in the preamble of the AA.[356] Some more general considerations of climate change can be found in Chapter 4 of Title VI ('other cooperation policies') of the AA, which specifically refers to climate action.

231. As explained in the general introduction of the monograph, in July 2017, Georgia acceded to the EnCT with a multilateral nature regulated by the Protocol Concerning the Accession of Georgia to the EnCT.[357] Like the AA, in its legal nature, the Protocol is an international treaty binding on Georgia, which enjoys supremacy vis-à-vis conflicting national laws. Nevertheless, the accession protocol does not specify any climate-specific EU law.

232. According to Article 10 of the Treaty, Georgia 'shall implement the *Acquis Communautaire* on energy in compliance with the timetable for the implementation of those measures set out in Annex I'.[358] Neither Annex I nor the more specific Accession Protocol includes climate-relevant *acquis* that is compulsory for Georgia. Instead, the legislation related to climate change comes into existence in the

354. For additional clarification, deadline becomes legally effective from the entry into the force of the AA (2016) and not from the date of signature (2014, i.e., provisional entry of the AA). *See*: https://ec.europa.eu/commission/presscorner/etail/en/IP_16_2369, accessed on 30 Mar. 2020.
355. Article 310 of the AA.
356. According to the international law, the preamble of an international agreement is not necessarily legally binding, but it very well reflects the essence and general nature of the agreement.
357. *See* I. Samkharadze, *The External Dimension of EU Energy Law and Policy: A Step Forward, but Towards What?*, Leuven Blog for Public Law, 22 Nov. 2019.
358. Article 10 of EnCT.

form of the EnC Recommendations, which are considered a 'soft law' instrument.[359] According to Article 76 of the Treaty, a recommendation has no binding force for CPs.[360] However, since the recommendations are made by the Ministerial Council, as the highest decision-making body of the EnC, Georgia still 'shall use their best endeavours to carry out recommendations' by virtue of its accession to the EnC.[361] Therefore, EnC recommendations should be highly respected and reflected accordingly within the domestic regulatory system.[362]

§2. THE COMMITMENTS STEMMING FROM THE AA AND ENC

233. Echoing above, four pieces of legislation are of particular importance for Georgia to take into account when harmonizing its climate legislative framework. Two of these acts are enshrined in Annex XXVII of the AA and another two are derived from EnC recommendations adopted by the Ministerial Council of the EnC.

234. The AA obligatory legislation covers Regulation (EC) No. 842/2006 on certain Fluorinated Greenhouse Gases (hereinafter 'F-gases Regulation'), which needs to be transposed into the Georgian legal system within five years after entry into force of the AA. It will directly contribute to combat climate change, as F-gases are controlled under the KP and thus are subject to the UNFCCC. The Regulation (EC) No. 1005/2009 on substances that deplete the ozone layer (hereinafter 'ODS Regulation') will also directly contribute to combat climate change, since, in addition to depleting the ozone layer, most Ozone Depleting Substances (ODS) controlled by the Montreal Protocol (MP) are also powerful GHGs.

235. Moreover, the AA defines the specific provisions under F-gases and ODS regulations that need to be incorporated within the stipulated timeframes. Therefore, Georgia is obliged to implement only certain provisions of the regulation, as explicitly listed in Annex XVII of the AA instead of incorporating the regulations in their entirety. This may, *inter alia*, include the compliance check to: (a) develop the legally binding instruments: drafting and adopting persistent national legislation and by-laws as well as amending the existing ones accordingly; (b) review licensing conditions and enforcement measures; (c) establish training and certification requirements (Article 5, F-gases Regulation) and a ban of the production of controlled substances (Article 4, ODS Regulation); (d) design the competent authorities, reporting systems and other non-legally binding tools, such as specific programmes contributing to the implementation process.

359. A. Konoplyanik, *The Role of the ECT in EU-Russia Energy Relations*, in *Research Handbook on EU Energy Law and Policy* 129 (R. Leal-Arcas & J. Wouters (eds), Edward Elgar 2017).

360. Article 76 of EnCT.

361. *Ibid.*

362. For more information *see*, I. Samkharadze, *Advancing National Climate Law: Is There Room for Mainstreaming EU Climate Action in Georgia?* Book Chapter, in *Experiencing Europeanization in the Black Sea and South Caucasus* 253–278 (O. Reisner, S. Türkeş-Kılıç & G. Gabrichidze (eds) AESC Book Series Volume No. 2, ibidem-Verlag 2021).

236. As for the EnC obligations, it is recommended that Georgia incorporates two pieces of Community in its legal corpus. The recommendation on preparing for the development of integrated National Energy and Climate Plans (NECPs) by the CPs of the EnC (EnC Recommendation on NECP) is encouraging the country to design an integrated climate and energy strategy for the implementation of the common targets. The recommendation on preparing for the implementation of Regulation (EU) 525/2013 on a mechanism for monitoring and reporting GHG emissions (EnC Recommendation on GHG monitoring and reporting) is facilitating the country to develop universal GHG monitoring and reporting system on the basis of the EU experience. The General Policy Guidelines on the 2030 targets for the CPs of the EnC should also be mentioned in this context.

Chapter 4. National Climate Legislative Framework

§1. THE OVERVIEW OF NATIONAL LEGISLATION RELEVANT TO CLIMATE CHANGE

237. As argued in the previous chapter, the legally binding AA provisions that are to be adopted in Georgia are stemming from the regulations, as legal acts of the EU. Albeit a regulation represents the secondary source of EU legislation, it is directly applicable and immediately enforceable law in all EU Member States as opposed to a directive, which needs to be transposed into national law.[363] This proposition, however, does not apply to Georgia, as an EU associate country. Namely, Georgia is a non-EU Member State and the EU regulations do not apply automatically in its domestic legal system. Therefore, in order to approximate the national legislation to the negotiated provisions of the EU regulations enshrined in the AA, the formal adoption of EU standards in the form of updating the existing legislation or adopting new ones (primary or secondary by-laws) is necessary. The regulations can be implemented by means of a variety of national legislative procedures depending on the specific subject matter.

238. Some legal foundations for the implementation of the regulations can, in principle, be found within the existing climate legislation in Georgia. However, they tend to be somewhat faulty and inadequate, which jeopardizes the legal harmonization process. As there is no single climate legal act in place, several sectoral laws and regulatory measures dealing with identified F-gas and ODS as well as NECP and GHG monitoring and reporting provisions should be found in different primary and secondary legislation. It is arguable whether there is sufficient regulatory space created in Georgia to accommodate the provisions that fully implement EU acts in the domestic legal system.

239. It is the 1996 Law of Georgia on Environmental Protection[364] to be invoked in the first place as a key primary national act providing the foundation for the establishment of national environmental legislation including the general reference to climate change (Article 51)[365] and protection of the ozone layer (Article 52).[366] The second significant primary domestic legal act to be scrutinized in this light is the 1999 Law of Georgia on Ambient Air Protection.[367] Its Chapter XV (Global and Regional Management of Ambient Air) contains the ODS relevance provisions (Article 54), containing five paragraphs, which have been amended in 2007, 2010, 2011, and 2013. Further to this, the Environmental Assessment Code was adopted

363. P. Burca & G. de Craig, *EU Law: Texts, Cases, and Materials* 107 (Oxford University Press 6th ed. 2015).
364. No. 519-1 Law of Georgia on Environmental Protection, 10 Dec. 1996.
365. Article 51, No. 519-1 Law of Georgia on Environmental Protection, 10 Dec. 1996.
366. Article 52, *ibid.*
367. No. 2116 Law of Georgia on Ambient Air Protection, 22 Jun. 1999.

on 1 June 2017, whereas the vulnerability of the activities to climate change and monitoring GHG emissions (Article 10) are mentioned accordingly.[368]

240. Apart from these key primary acts, several other secondary laws are in place in the country, which support transposition of the afore-reviewed EU climate *acquis* nationally. These acts vary to a large degree including the resolution of the Parliament of Georgia[369] and the Governmental decrees.[370] It should also be mentioned that national policy documents and sectoral strategies play a crucial role currently in forming the national climate regulatory framework. The National Strategy on Sustainable Development Goals,[371] the Social-Economic Development Strategy of Georgia 2020,[372] the National Environment Action Programme (2017–2021),[373] as well as Climate Action Plan and National Renewable Energy Action Plan & NEEAP[374] – under preparation – should also be cited in this context.

§2. The Implementation of the AA Climate Acquis into Georgian Legislation

241. In relation to the EU F-gas regulation, it should be mentioned that the primary objective of the regulation is to reduce the emissions of the fluorinated gases covered by the KP.[375] However, what needs to be emphasized is that these gases (HFCs, PFCs and SF6)[376] are not produced in Georgia. They are imported for domestic consumption and, therefore, emissions are generated mostly from their use. Although as a non-Annex I party to UNFCCC, Georgia does have a binding emission reduction commitment under KP, controlling F-gases could contribute to overall measures reducing GHG emissions. Given this, aligning the domestic legislation to the EU F-gas Regulation does not only come in conformity with the AA implementation but it also contributes to the UNFCCC process.

242. There are certain national provisions in Georgia that correspond to the AA, but their general nature does not set out any specific measures related to the

368. Article 10(3), N890-IIS Environmental Assessment Code, 1 Sep. 2017.
369. For example, No. 828 The Resolution of the Parliament of Georgia 'On Harmonization of Georgian Legislation with the EU Law', 2 Sep. 1997.
370. No. 302 Decree of the government of Georgia on national requirements for a mandatory certification system and training for refrigeration and air conditioning technicians (22 Jun. 2017).
371. No. 2328 Ordinance of the Government of Georgia on approval of the National Strategy of the Sustainable Development Goals, 12 Nov. 2019.
372. No. 400 Ordinance of the Government of Georgia on approval of Socio-Economic Development Strategy of Georgia – 'Georgia 2020' and Associated Activities, 17 Jun. 2014.
373. The full document available at: http://extwprlegs1.fao.org/docs/pdf/geo180258.pdf, accessed on 12 Dec. 2019.
374. *See* the 2nd BUR available at: https://www4.unfccc.int/sites/SubmissionsStaging/NationalReports/Documents/03268145_Georgia-BUR2-1-2019.06.13_BUR2_2019_Eng.pdf, accessed on 12 Jan. 2020.
375. Article 1, EU F-gas Regulation.
376. *See* the detailed list of the gases in the respective Annex of the EU F-gas Regulation.

climate-protecting F-gas framework. It must also be emphasized that a good number of specific amendments have already been applied in the domestic legal system, which ensures partial implementation of the F-gas Regulation requirements. Apart from already integrated amendments, the additional amendments are now approved by the Parliament. In this context, an amendment to the Ambient Air Protection Law registered on 10 April 2019 and adopted on 20 May 2020 should be mentioned.[377] It does not only contain some of the specific provisions itself to implement the EU F-gas regulation, but it also indicates (Article 12(5)) on the technical regulation that needs to be prepared and adopted in due course. The latter will detail a legal pathway towards the full implementation of the F-gas regulation.

243. With regards to the ODS system, it is widely recognized that continued emissions of ODS cause significant damage to the ozone layer. Against this proposition, the objective of the ODS Regulation is to fulfil the obligations of the MP on substances that deplete the ozone layer, to which Georgia is a party. It thus lays down the rules on the production, import, export, placing on the market, use, recovery, recycling, reclamation and destruction of substances that deplete the ozone layer, on the reporting of information related to those substances and on the import, export, placing on the market and use of products and equipment containing or relying on those substances.[378]

244. As for the EU ODS Regulation implementation progress, the scrutiny of national legislation indicates that the starting point of the ODS Regulation transposition in Georgian national legislation was in a better position in comparison with F-gas Regulation. Namely, the competent authority (i.e., Ministry of Environmental Protection and Agriculture) has for quite some time been already designated by virtue of Article 13 of the Law of Environmental Protection[379] and Article 54 of the Law of Ambient Air Protection.[380] The ban on the production of controlled substances (Article 4 ODS Regulation) has also been in place before the signature of the AA according to Article 52(1) of the Law of Environmental Protection and Article 54(1) of another.

§3. THE IMPLEMENTATION OF THE EnC CLIMATE ACQUIS INTO GEORGIAN LEGISLATION

245. NECPs are the new framework within which EU Member States must plan, in an integrated manner, their climate and energy objectives, targets, policies and measures to the European Commission (EC).[381] Despite the fact that NECPs are originated within the EU Member States' context, they have a spillover effect on the countries partnering with the EU. EnC Recommendation on NECP is a prime

377. No. 07-2/332/9 Amendment to the Law of Georgia on Ambient Air Protection.
378. Article 1, EU ODS Regulation.
379. Article 13, No. 2116 Law of Georgia on Ambient Air Protection, 22 Jun. 1999.
380. Article 54(4), *ibid.*
381. *See* National Energy and Climate Plans (NECPs) https://energy.ec.europa.eu/topics/energy-strategy/national-energy-and-climate-plans-necps_en, accessed on 20 Feb. 2022.

example of that highly encouraging Georgia to originally design and submit its Plan by October 2020.[382] In fact, the Georgian NECP has not been submitted by October 2020, but it is expected to be finalized by the end of 2023.[383]

246. According to Article 1 of the EnC Recommendation on NECP, 'the Contracting Parties should prepare the analytical, institutional and regulatory preconditions for the development and adoption of integrated NECPs for the period from 2021 to 2030'.[384] NECPs should be addressing the five dimensions of the Energy Union[385] and should ensure coherence with the PA as well as other possible long-term energy and climate targets for 2030.

247. What is more relevant, the landmark energy sector reform laws have recently been adopted in Georgia mandated by Third Energy Package[386] substituting existing energy market framework. Namely, Law of Georgia on Energy and Water Supply was enacted on 20 December 2019[387] and Law of Georgia on Encouraging the Production and Use of Energy from Renewable Sources was also passed on 20 December 2019.[388] It is expected these laws to create the framework not only for modernizing the energy market accommodating the EU energy law key principles,[389] but establishing the legal grounds for long-term energy strategy and planning. How does NECP fit under the framework law and does this latter explicitly refer to it?

248. Article 7 of the recently adopted framework energy law,[390] specifically indicates that the 'State Energy Policy may encompass the integrated NECP of Georgia addressing dimensions of the energy security and solidarity, energy markets, decarbonization, innovation and competitiveness in the energy sector, and moderation of energy demand'. This can very well be considered a strong legal declaratory foundation paving the way towards actual preparation of the NECP also containing certain references to the regional cooperation. On top of that, the recently

382. *See* Policy Guidelines on the development of National Energy and Climate Plans under Recommendation 2018/01/MC-EnC, June 2018.
383. Energy Community Secretariat Annual Implementation Report, Georgia (climate), November 2021, p. 70.
384. Article 1 of the 2018/1/MC-EnC on preparing for the development of integrated NECPs by the Contracting Parties of the Energy Community.
385. (1) Energy security, solidarity and trust. (2) A fully integrated energy market. (3) Energy efficiency. (4) Climate action – decarbonizing economy. (5) Research, innovation and competitiveness. For detailed analysis, *see* EU Commission Communication 'A Framework Strategy for a Resilient Energy Union with a Forward-Looking Climate Change Policy'.
386. For more information, *see*: https://ec.europa.eu/energy/en /topics/markets-and-consumers/market-legislation/third-energy-package, accessed on 22 Sep. 2020.
387. No. 5646-RS Law of Georgia on Energy and Water Supply, 20 Dec. 2019.
388. No. 5652 Law of Georgia on Promoting the Production and Use of Energy from Renewable Sources, 20 Dec. 2019.
389. *See* I. Samkharadze, *The EU Energy Law External Action and Its Impact Assessment on Municipal Georgian Legislation*, 1 Tbilisi State U. L. Rev. 241–257 (2018).
390. Article 7(3), No. 5646-RS Law of Georgia on Energy and Water Supply, 20 Dec. 2019.

passed Renewable Energy Law should additionally be mentioned establishing the conditions for the approval of the National Renewable Energy Action Plan.[391]

249. At the time of writing, however, the implementation of Georgia's NECP has not been completed. As enshrined in the Annual Implementation Report 2021, 'Georgia's draft NECP is currently being discussed with wider stakeholder groups based on an agreement under the Namakhvani mediation process. Finalization is expected in early 2022'.[392] The same document assesses the overall implementation status with 62%.[393]

250. As for the EnC Recommendation on GHG monitoring and reporting, Georgia is inclined to prepare the legal and institutional preconditions for the implementation of the core elements of Regulation No. 525/2013[394] of the EU. The legal analysis shows that the Regulation is not transposed into national legislation, but two general provisions have been found in primary national legislation in line with the requirements of the Regulation. Article 51 of Law of Environmental Protection establishes the basic obligations of the entities in the field of climate change,[395] such as reducing greenhouse gases in the atmosphere, but there is no reporting obligation per se.

251. This article creates only a general legal foundation for GHG monitoring and reporting and it does not specify the mechanisms for providing the data to the collecting entities. It rather makes a reference to a legal framework for the protection of the climate from global changes within the jurisdiction of Georgia. Article 1 of the Law of Official Statistics can also be mentioned in this context with regard to country's compliance with the United Nations (UN) Fundamental Principles of Official Statistics and the European Statistics Code of Practice. Nevertheless, it should be claimed that the 'core elements'[396] of the EU 525/2013 Regulation remain ill-regulated in the national legal system. There is no sophisticated national monitoring and reporting legal setup in place and the major gaps are associated with failure of the legislative framework and institutional structures to monitor and report the GHG in a systematic manner.

252. What complicates the process is that the main sources of obtaining necessary information are LEPL, Environmental Information and Education Centre

391. Article 4, No. 5652 Law of Georgia on Promoting the Production and Use of Energy from Renewable Sources, 20 Dec. 2019.
392. Energy Community Secretariat Annual Implementation Report, Georgia (climate), November 2021.
393. *Ibid.*, p. 70.
394. Regulation (EU) No. 525/2013 of The European Parliament and of The Council of 21 May 2013 on a mechanism for monitoring and reporting greenhouse gas emissions and for reporting other information at national and Union level relevant to climate change and repealing Decision No. 280/2004/EC.
395. Article 51, No. 519-1 Law of Georgia on Environmental Protection, 10 Dec. 1996.
396. For example, Low-carbon development strategies (Art. 4); National inventory systems (Arts 5–14); Biennial reports and national communications (Art. 18).

(EIEC) and National Statistics Office of Georgia (GeoStat),[397] but there is no legal obligation for data providers to transfer any information to EIEC and GeoStat. The information is collected in a random manner with no sustainable reporting system and documents are prepared on an ad hoc basis.[398] The collecting entities receive information from a wide variety of organizations, such as local governmental authorities (including municipalities), subordinated departments, private sector, Civil Society Organizations and international donors. These entities are often reluctant to provide sensitive data that can cause misconceptions about the final results.

397. Based on the Memorandum of Understanding with the Ministry of Environmental Protection and Agriculture of Georgia signed in 2014.

398. For more detailed analysis, *see* Background Paper on a Legal Setup for MRV in Georgia prepared under GIZ 'Information Matters' Project (PN: 2012.9020.4-003).

Conclusions

253. This monograph primarily focuses on desk review, legal research, comparative analysis, *acquis* implementation comparison and benchmarking to map the state of the art in regard to energy law and policy framework in Georgia. Based on what has been examined, the monograph concludes that Georgian energy law is in the phase of rapid evolution to serve the energy transition process towards a more market-oriented energy sector. Although the country has already implemented a number of key reforms to accelerate its transformation from a post-Soviet republic to a free-enterprise economy, its energy market framework still remains heavily influenced by the Soviet legacy. This is most evident in poor performance in terms of competitiveness and the absence of a regulatory landscape to stimulate smart energy solutions.

254. Nevertheless, Georgian energy legislation reform and the creation of a stable, more competitive and transparent legal framework is an irreversible process. As described closely above, the country is bound to a great amount of EU energy and climate *acquis* deriving from bilateral and multilateral treaties. The latest EnC annual implementation report (November 2021), assessing Georgia's progress with respect to AA and EnC requirements, finds that the country has demonstrated its willingness to establish itself as a successful energy partner with the EU. The evaluation of Georgia's compliance against the *acquis* shows some promising results despite the fact that the majority of the implementation deadlines set by the EnC Accession Protocol are yet to expire.

255. As outlined above, the adoption of the framework energy law – 'Law of Georgia on Energy and Water Supply' – covering almost all aspects of energy regulation is a key milestone in this course of reform encapsulating the provisions on unbundling, TPA, regulatory authorities, cross-border exchange in electricity and gas, consumer protection and public service obligations. Besides, the recently enacted 'Law of Georgia on Encouraging the Production and Use of Energy from Renewable Sources' as well as 'Law on Energy Efficiency' and the 'Law on Energy Performance of Buildings' projected Georgia's green energy endeavours ranging from uptaking the share of renewable energy in the gross final energy consumption to receiving significant investments in public building renovation programmes. These highlights certainly indicate Georgian energy law progress, but energy transition overall remains to be supported further with more sophisticated mechanisms for strengthening energy and climate governance in close cooperation with the EU and EnC Secretariat.

256. It is anticipated that future development of Georgia's energy law will largely be driven by the EU's flagship European Green Deal (EGD) initiative as a new growth strategy transforming the EU into a fair and prosperous society, with a resource-efficient and competitive economy where there are no net emissions of GHGs by 2050.[399] EGD, which maps the state of the art with regard to climate-neutral Europe is the latest climate action blueprint and Europe's much-awaited decarbonization pathway by 2050.

257. Clearly, the EGD is not a European vision only. Instead, its geography is much larger reflecting on the EU's strategies to engage with its neighbours, allies and other partners. At the time of writing, EGD and its subsequent processes and legislation (incl. EU Climate Law and 'Fit for 55 Package') do not have direct applicability to Georgia. It affects in an indirect manner via using the EU's soft power elements and the conditionality policy in meeting Georgia's EU association goals. It, nevertheless, should be expected that Georgia shapes its forthcoming energy and climate legislative framework including new trends of decarbonization (e.g., hydrogen) in line with the EGD policies as catalyzed by bilateral and multilateral agreements with the EU.

258. Following the EU Association track and membership in the Energy Community, Georgia is in the process of implementing significant reforms in the Georgian energy sector. This is mainly inspired by gradual alignment with the negotiated EU energy and climate acquis as explained above. The reform is seeking to transform the Georgian energy market from a bilateral monthly settlement and low-competition, trade system to an EU-style open market with liberalized, competitive price-setting mechanisms, balanced responsibility and sustainability approaches.

259. Uncovering more of what is to be seen under the open energy market approach, one may need to think of the contemporary energy law principles of the EU of non-discriminatory and transparent nature. A future electricity market design of Georgia should be mainstreamed with unbundled transmission and DSOs, a strong independent regulator, the legal regulation of public service obligations and protection of vulnerable customers. This must be strongly embedded into the development of RES and their support mechanisms as requested by the updated framework of renewable energy laws, including implementation of market-based support mechanisms' deployment. It also needs to be 'teamed up' with the facilitation of energy efficiency as ensured by the recently adopted regulatory framework of energy efficiency, which includes a horizontal (cross-sectoral) policy that impacts public and private sectors and a wide variety of other crucial energy efficiency topics.

399. Communication from the Commission to the European Parliament, the European Council, the Council, the European Economic and Social Committee and the Committee of the Regions the European Green Deal COM/2019/640 final.

Selected Bibliography

Background Paper on a Legal Setup for MRV in Georgia prepared under GIZ 'Information Matters' Project (PN: 2012.9020.4-003).

Blockmans, S., et al. 'Integrity and Judicial Reform on Trial'. In, *The Struggle for Good Governance in Eastern Europe*, edited by M. Emerson, D. Cenusa, T. Kovziridze & V. Movchan. Centre for European Policy Studies, 2018.

Blockmans, S. & V.B. Vooren. *Revitalizing the European Neighborhood Economic Community: The Case for Legally Binding Sectoral Multilateralism.* Working Paper, Leuven Centre for Global Governance Studies 91 (2012).

Burca, P. & Gráinne de Craig. *EU Law: Texts, Cases, and Materials.* 6th edn. Oxford University Press, 2015.

Emerson, M. & T. Kovziridze (eds). *Deepening EU-Georgian Relations What Why and How?*. 2nd edn. Centre for European Policy Studies, 2018.

Konoplyanik, A., 'The Role of the ECT in EU-Russia Energy Relations'. In *Research Handbook on EU Energy Law and Policy*, edited by R. Leal-Arcas & J. Wouters. Edward Elgar, 2017.

Samkharadze, I. 'Changing Architecture of Georgian Renewable Energy Normative System: The Dos and Don'ts from the European Union', 30, *European Energy and Environmental Law Review* 94–103 (2021).

Samkharadze, I. 'Advancing National Climate Law: Is there Room for Mainstreaming EU Climate Action in Georgia?' Book chapter In: *Experiencing Europeanization in the Black Sea and South Caucasus*, edited by O. Reisner, S. Türkeş-Kılıç & G. Gabrichidze. AESC Book Series Volume No. 2, ibidem-Verlag, pp. 253–278, 2021.

Samkharadze, I. 'Europeanization of Energy Law and Policy Beyond the Member States: The Case of Georgia'. *Elsevier Energy Policy Journal* 130 (2019).

Samkharadze, I. *Text of the Constitution of Georgia.* International Encyclopedia of Laws: Constitutional Law, Wolters Kluwer, Kluwer Law International, Suppl. Vol. 154 (2020).

Samkharadze, I. 'The Impact of EU Energy Law External Action on Georgian Legislation', 1 *Tbilisi State University Law Review* (2018).

Samkharadze, I. 'The External Dimension of EU Energy Law and Policy: A Step Forward, but Towards What?'. Leuven Blog for Public Law (22 November 2019).

Quintavalla, Alberto, Franz Kienzl, and Irakli Samkharadze. ″The human right to energy: drawing lessons from the development of the human right to water.″ Journal of Human Rights and the Environment 14.1 (2023): 49-66.

Social-economic Development Strategy of Georgia 'GEORGIA 2020'.

Selected Bibliography

The Energy Strategy of Georgia 2020–2030.
Third National Communication of Georgia to the UN Framework Convention on Climate Change (UNFCCC), Tbilisi.
Tsurtsumia, T. & S. Janelidze. *Obligations in the Field of Energy Defined by the Protocol of Georgia's Accession to the Founding Agreement of the Energy Union*. Konrad Adenauer Stiftung, 2019.

Websites

www.unfccc.int
www.esco.ge
www.parliament.ge
www.law.kuleuven.be/pub/en
www.energy-community.org/
www.caneurope.org
www.ec.europa.eu
www.gov.ge
www.iea.org

Table of Legislation

Table of Legislation

Index

The numbers here refer to paragraph numbers.

www.ingramcontent.com/pod-product-compliance
Lightning Source LLC
Chambersburg PA
CBHW071352230926
51846CB00002B/529
9789403534978